WORD
KNOWLEDGE

A Vocabulary Teacher's Handbook

Cheryl Boyd Zimmerman

OXFORD
UNIVERSITY PRESS

OXFORD
UNIVERSITY PRESS

198 Madison Avenue
New York, NY 10016 USA

Great Clarendon Street, Oxford ox2 6DP UK

Oxford University Press is a department of the University of Oxford.
It furthers the University's objective of excellence in research, scholarship,
and education by publishing worldwide in

Oxford New York
Auckland Cape Town Dar es Salaam Hong Kong Karachi
Kuala Lumpur Madrid Melbourne Mexico City Nairobi
New Delhi Shanghai Taipei Toronto

With offices in
Argentina Austria Brazil Chile Czech Republic France Greece
Guatemala Hungary Italy Japan Poland Portugal Singapore
South Korea Switzerland Thailand Turkey Ukraine Vietnam

OXFORD and OXFORD ENGLISH are registered trademarks of
Oxford University Press.

© Oxford University Press 2009

Database right Oxford University Press (maker)

Library of Congress Cataloging-in-Publication Data

Zimmerman, Cheryl Boyd, 1950–
    Word knowledge: a vocabulary teacher's handbook / Cheryl Boyd Zimmerman.
        p. cm.
    Includes bibliographical references and index.
    ISBN 978-0-19-470393-2 (pbk.)
    1. English language—Study and teaching—Foreign speakers. 2. Vocabulary—Study and
teaching—Handbooks, manuals, etc. I. Title.
    PE1128.A2.Z56 2008
    428.2'4—dc22

                                                                2007046269

Executive Publishing Manager: Laura Le Dréan
Senior Managing Editor: Patricia O'Neill
Senior Development Editor: Dena Daniel
Design Director: Robert Carangelo
Design Manager: Maj-Britt Hagsted
Cover design: Stacy Merlin
Image Editor: Robin Fadool
Project Coordinator: Sarah Dentry
Manufacturing Manager: Shanta Persaud
Manufacturing Controller: Eve Wong

ISBN: 978 0 19 470393 2

Printed in Hong Kong

10 9 8 7 6 5 4 3 2 1

ACKNOWLEDGMENTS
Cover art: Stone / Getty Images: Ryan McVay

Contents

Preface

A handbook is a manual, guide, or reference book designed to make a complex task clear. We turn to a handbook when we take on a new task or try to improve our performance in a familiar one. This vocabulary handbook for teachers, written for both new and experienced teachers of English as a second or foreign language, is designed to help tease apart the complex process of vocabulary learning and teaching and to provide ideas for addressing learners' needs. Its premise is that teachers are best prepared to guide students when they themselves respect the enormous task of word learning and are aware of the factors involved in knowing a word.

This book was made possible by many people who appreciate the challenges presented to the vocabulary learner and teacher. First, I am grateful for the support of Oxford University Press, beginning with Pietro Alongi, who recognized the need for such a book and helped initiate this project, and continuing with Amy Cooper, whose editorial skills facilitated my writing and gave me a stellar example of how to effectively guide writers. In the end it was Dena Daniel who pulled the project together with careful reading, constructive feedback, and administrative finesse.

This project was further facilitated by a sabbatical leave provided by California State University, Fullerton, and by the support of several colleagues in the Department of Modern Languages and Literatures who worked beyond the call of duty in my absence: Nathan Carr, Janet Eyring, Juan Carlos Gallego, and Marjorie Tussing. Thanks also to those colleagues who took the time to comment on portions of the manuscript: Linda Andersen, Reyes Fidalgo, and Norbert Schmitt. Arline Burgmeier read early drafts too rough to give to anyone but a very good friend. Special thanks go to Margaret Plenert for her generous and insightful help with every stage of this project. Valuable examples were contributed by Amanda Boyd, Deborah Boyd, Julia Boyd, Laura Boyd, Marshall Boyd, Amy Cooper, Dena Daniel, Nathan Handel, and Lynda Zimmerman.

In this book about the challenges of word learning, the greatest debt is owed to the English language learners who have shared their word learning experiences with me and have helped me recognize the intricacies of word knowledge. Most of the examples used in this book were gathered from English language learners either by me or by my graduate students at California State University, Fullerton. I am most grateful to these graduate students for their insightful data collection: Justine Ancheta, Rhonda Cisneros, Priscilla Constantine, Tina Constantinou, Daniel Cook, Thu Thi Hoai Do, Natalya Dollar, Robby Edwards, Richard Emenjian, Ann Hiramatsu, Jennifer Hohri, Andre Hsu, Amanda Jerome, Liza Lockhart, Susi Lopez, Machiko Miki, Futoshi Nakagawa, Anneke Painter, Avery Quatro, Cecilia Salzer, Gail Schwartz, Dina Skrabalak, Jillanne Thomas, Hope Vigil, Dolores Winter, Manasawee Wongpradu, and Tina Wu.

Finally, one who is particularly aware of the challenges of word learning is my patient husband, who has long supported my work and has endured more than his share of discussions about how words operate and why we use them the way we do. Thanks, David.

Introduction

I still have the ideas, Walter,
but I can't find the words to clothe them.

(from Winston Churchill to Walter Monckton)

BACKGROUND

Stop for a minute and marvel at the wonder of your own word knowledge. Sure, we all wish we knew more words than we do, and we would often like to express ourselves better. But consider what you *do* know. As an educated adult, you probably know approximately 50,000 words and are able to use about 90% of them.[1] Even more impressive than the number of words is what you know about each one. For example, you know enough about spelling and pronunciation to recognize and use a word both in writing and speech, even in cases of great irregularity (e.g., *tough, bough, thorough, thought,* and *ghetto*). Furthermore, you frequently make sense of sentences in which words have different meanings but the same form:

> The hospital wouldn't admit an <u>invalid</u> with an <u>invalid</u> insurance card.
> Since there is no time like the <u>present</u>, he thought it was time to <u>present</u> the <u>present</u>.

In fact, there are many intricate details involved in what you know about word meaning. At some level, whether conscious or not, you know that the word *lose* means "to be unable to find something," and you normally expect to see it used literally in reference to such things as car keys and cell phones. But when you encounter usages that don't fit the literal definition, you adapt what you know about the word. You may not even notice this ability to apply your knowledge to many different usages. Consider the variety of meanings to navigate when you encounter *lose*:

lose a tooth	lose a turn	lose money
lose weight	lose a loved one	lose face
lose a place in line	lose sleep	lose a cop

Lose is not an exception. Confusing word meanings dominate the media (e.g., *How green is the White House?*), conversation (e.g., *I feel like soup today.*), and all aspects of our lives. For example, a recent conference for international students announced, "A light breakfast will be provided." The students were left to decide which meaning of *light* was intended. Did it refer to the breakfast's color, weight, calorie content, or the amount of food served?

Word meaning is not the only arbitrary feature of language that demands your considerable skill with words. Other features are the use of word classes (e.g., I can *lunch* with my family, but I cannot *dinner* with them.) and word formation (e.g., *I am delightful to be here.*). Whereas the first sentence below shows the proper use of an affix to change the part of speech, the second one does not.

When my relatives visit, we are hospitable to them.

*When my relatives visit, we hospitalize them.[†]

The task of word learning is daunting, and it warrants great respect. But it's not impossible. If we acknowledge that learning a word is incremental and that it happens one step at a time, we will approach it realistically as a process rather than a single act of memorization. The various aspects of knowing a word (e.g., meaning, collocation, grammatical features, word parts, and appropriateness) are understood gradually, over time, as a result of seeing a word and using it.[2] For example, when you learn the word *marble*, you need to know its meaning ("a hard attractive stone that is used to make statues and parts of buildings"), its part of speech (noun), and its collocations (you *make* or *carve* something out of marble). The writer of the following sentence knows all of those aspects of the word, but something is missing:

*The Taj Mahal is made from white marbles.

[†]The use of an asterisk (*) indicates that a sentence is ungrammatical or unacceptable in standard use.

Marble is an uncountable noun. This is another aspect of word knowledge that is essential for accurate usage. Unbeknownst to the writer, *marble* takes on a completely different meaning when we use it as a countable noun (marbles: the toys used in a children's game).

As teachers, we cannot expect to anticipate every idiosyncrasy of every word or every gap in a word learner's knowledge, but we can develop skills that will make our insights valuable to the word learner. In this sense, a teacher of English language learners[††] must become a learner along with the students, persistently on the lookout for insights about why we use words as we do. This can happen in a classroom where authentic language is enjoyed, word awareness is encouraged, and "errors" are seen as opportunities to better understand words.

A CLOSER LOOK AT WORD LEARNING AND TEACHING

1 Word Consciousness[3]

If you have ever wondered why a *toothbrush* isn't called a **teethbrush* or why *silverware* can be made of plastic, you have shown some word consciousness—an awareness and appreciation of words and the ability to reflect on their use. Words are fascinating! This idea has been popularized by Richard Lederer, author of many books about the English language. Lederer points out that words are less straightforward than we might think:

> We drive in the parkway and park in the driveway.
> We play at recitals but recite at plays.
> Quicksand takes you down slowly.
> Boxing rings are square.

These examples demonstrate that there are some patterns that facilitate word learning (e.g., *teachers teach* and *stingers sting*) and others that get in the way (e.g., *grocers* don't **groce* and *fingers* don't **fing*).[4] Word consciousness is an alertness to words, quirks and all. It is a helpful and often entertaining reminder that language is human, not always consistent, and often confusing.

Word consciousness is valuable in academic pursuits; in fact, it is "essential for comprehending the language of schooling."[5] Word

[††]This term refers to those learning English as a second or additional language.

learners benefit when classroom discussions and activities regularly feature discussions of register (e.g., *Would you use the word* sibling *when you talk to your friend? What other word might you use?*), the precision of words (e.g., *How is* fraudulent *different from dishonest?*), and the differences in word choices in speaking and writing (e.g., *You might use the word* kids *in a conversation. What word would you use in writing?*). Research has shown that simple discussions like these are very valuable to word learners. For example, in a seven-year study of the development of word consciousness in elementary school children, teachers used regular class discussions and practice exercises to alert learners to word usage. Students also had frequent opportunities to experiment. The positive results included an increase in the learners' accurate use of words and their motivation to use new words.[6]

Answering questions about why we use words as we do can be very difficult for a proficient speaker of a language. In the interest of fluency, we often don't notice the reasons behind our word choices; we are guided by an unconscious intuition. For example, many proficient speakers of English would correctly recognize that something is wrong with the following sentences, but they may not know how to identify the problems.

*The boys made their homework.

*The volcano wasn't working.

*The man is six feet high.

Word consciousness would lead a teacher to wonder why these sentences sound wrong and then to look for an explanation. In fact, the reason lies in the principle of **collocation**, or the tendency of certain words to occur with certain other words. Most of us never learned this principle consciously, but we know that we *do* homework, volcanoes *erupt*, and a man is six feet *tall*.

Proficient speakers might also be unaware of the many words and phrases with misleading word parts. For example, *rugged* is unrelated to *rug*, just as *stingy* is unrelated to *sting*. The term *over-the-counter drugs* is confusing because it refers to drugs that don't require prescriptions, whereas the only counter in most drug stores is used for prescription drugs. In addition, while *a lot* and *a few* are opposites, *quite a lot* and *quite a few* mean the same thing. Word formation can also be misleading. The opposite of *careless* is *careful* and the opposite of *harmless* is *harmful*, but the pattern does not hold for the opposites of *strapless* and *tireless*. Or consider the skill involved in interpreting the meanings of *crack* as used in the phrases *crack the case, crack a whip*, and *crack down on crime.*[7]

The premise of this book is that word consciousness is a critical skill to develop, first for vocabulary teachers, and then for their students. It will enable learners to improve their use of words by making insightful observations about words in authentic use. A key aspect of word consciousness is acknowledging the extensiveness of what it means to know a word. That is, word consciousness includes a growing understanding of the many layers of word knowledge.

2 The Layers of Word Knowledge

To know a word means to know a great deal about it. This view is the premise of many current theories and learning materials. The concept is credited to Paul Nation, a widely published and highly respected researcher and practitioner in second-language vocabulary study. Nation proposed a breakdown of the types of knowledge involved in knowing a word, including its written and spoken forms, grammatical patterns, collocations, frequency, appropriateness, and meaning, including concept and associations.[8]

In this book, the types or features of word knowledge are likened to layers, which are added incrementally, in no particular order. The goal of the learner is to glean information from each encounter with a word, and to gradually add layer after layer of knowledge until a word is understood and can be used with ease. Effective word learners continue to notice more and more about word use, and acquire more layers of word knowledge as they encounter words again and again. The following chart illustrates what a complicated task this is:

LAYERS OF WORD KNOWLEDGE	EXAMPLES
Meaning	
positive / negative connotation	The woman is slim / skinny.
degree ("strength" of a word)	*Student records are annihilated after five years.
Collocations	
fixed phrases	*Large sums of people were present.
preposition use	*They all discriminated me because of my accent.

LAYERS OF WORD KNOWLEDGE	EXAMPLES
Grammatical Features	
passive / active verbs	*I am fit by a size 9 dress.
verb complements	*I like to ski because I enjoy to go fast.
count / uncountable nouns	*No dopes are allowed on this campus. (intended as a reference to drugs)
parts of speech	*It is rude to bubble the gum in someone's face.
Word Parts	
right meaning, wrong suffix	*The car was spewing exhaustion.
word building gone awry	*There is great bondage between my grandmother and me.
Register / Appropriate Forms	
formal / informal	What's happening, dude? (employee to boss)
polite or people-sensitive / impolite	Physically challenged / Crippled people can live active lives.
direct / euphemistic	I heard that your uncle died / passed away.

Word learning is further complicated by the fact that each word poses different types of difficulties. For example, while collocation explains the challenge of using the word *suicide* (we say *commit suicide*, not **do suicide*), the multiple meanings of *lose* pose another type of difficulty (*lose car keys, lose weight, lose sleep,* etc.). Awareness of such differences is critical to successful word learning.

KEY CONSIDERATIONS FOR THE CLASSROOM

Every language teacher is a vocabulary teacher. Whether the focus of your class is vocabulary, reading, integrated skills, or advanced writing, learners will benefit when you help raise their word consciousness and when you draw attention to the layers of word knowledge. Here are some guidelines for vocabulary teaching in a variety of classroom settings.

1 Be Selective about the Words You Target

There will never be enough time to teach every word that your students will need. In fact, doing so would be boring and inefficient. Some words are easy to pick up from the context of a reading, a short explanation, or a translation. Others are learned through natural exposure. Relatively few of the words that students need can be covered in classroom instruction. Words that merit precious class time are high-frequency words that relate to useful topics and that pose particular challenges. For example, consider this sentence:

> Currently, 20 U.S. states or municipalities impose taxes on cell-phone users.

You could easily clarify the word *municipalities* with a brief explanation or translation; however, you might want to spend more time on *impose* in an academic English class if the word has value for the topics you are covering. You might also choose to focus on this word because of its other features: it is a transitive verb, completed by the noun *taxes*; it has a slightly negative connotation (you would never say **impose a tax rebate*); and it often is followed by the collocate *on*.

To begin, select only a few words for vocabulary instruction (5–10 words for a single lesson). It takes only a short time to explain a word, but expect to take considerable time for students to practice using the word, negotiate meaning, and reflect and comment on word use. As a general rule, it is more useful to explain, recycle, and practice a small number of well-chosen words than it is to give a longer list a quick treatment. Make your word selection based on the following criteria:

Frequency

Target high-frequency words because they will naturally occur both inside and outside the classroom, providing the repeated exposures that learners need. Some frequency lists can help you identify the first, second, and third thousand most frequent words in common use; others list the most frequent words in academic materials.[9] It is also important to trust your own good sense about which words your students will encounter often or otherwise find useful. For example, you may want to cover words that frequently occur in your classroom, even if they aren't listed among the words of greatest frequency (e.g., *abbreviate, instruction, quote, state, verify*).

Salience

Words are salient when they are central to a given context. Make good use of the contexts you choose by selecting target words that are needed, first, for comprehension of a text, and later, for its analysis, summary, or discussion. For example, a study using the movie *Raiders of the Lost Ark* found that learners made significant gains with the words *chanting, windshield,* and *secret.* Although each word had occurred less than three times in the movie, these words are of central importance to the story.[10]

Learners' academic or career goals

As you select words for a given group, consider the students' personal goals and academic aspirations. For students with academic goals, academic vocabulary is critical.[11] Academic words help learners express complex thoughts with precision. These words are difficult to learn because they occur with low frequency in conversational language. They take time to master and merit classroom attention. In David Corson's seminal book on academic word knowledge, he suggests that the best way to aid the learning of academic words is to engage learners in "motivated, serious conversations which demand those meanings in use."[12] Discussions and activities with this goal characterize effective vocabulary classrooms. Such activities are quite different from memorizing lists or filling in blanks.

A word's learning burden

Some words are more difficult to master than others. A word's learning burden—the amount of effort needed to master it—is influenced greatly by the learner's first language. The learning burden is relatively light for words that behave in a way that is similar to the learner's first language and heavy for those that behave differently. The learning burden is bound to be heavy for patterns or features that don't appear in the first language.

Other factors that influence the difficulty of word learning[13]:

- word length
- pronunciation
- abstractness (concrete words are easier)
- inflectional complexity (irregular plural and past tense forms are harder than regular forms)

- derivational complexity (e.g., *discourse* can be mistakenly understood as "without direction")
- parts of speech (nouns and verbs are easier)
- idiomaticity (*to decide* is easier than *to make up one's mind*)
- multiple meanings (e.g., *bank* and *neck*)

The main point to remember is this: the more predictable a word's form and meaning are, the lighter the learning burden.[14] Words with a lighter learning burden require less classroom time.

2 Be Selective about the Information You Present

The word learning process is indeed daunting. As we have seen, it includes learning about a word's meaning(s), collocations, register and appropriateness, pronunciation, spelling, and more. Pre-teaching words before learners practice them is useful when your comments are brief and carefully focused on the information that is most important for the task at hand. Remember that hearing too many details is both boring and confusing. Consider which information would best enable your students to use the word in the particular activity. You might find it helpful to first think carefully about your own use of the word. What do you have to know to use it? Does it have an irregular form? Does it have any common collocates? If it's a verb, can you follow it with an object, a *that*-clause, or a prepositional phrase? Features of language such as these will be explained and practiced throughout this book.

To further develop your ability to give concise and perceptive explanations, pay attention to student errors. Learn to identify the things that cause the most difficulty. Remember that providing succinct and helpful explanations and good examples is an art as well as a skill, and it will take some time to learn how to do it well.

3 Provide Adequate Repetition

Word learning is incremental. In order for a new word to be retained, it must be encountered again (and again) before it is forgotten.[15] How many encounters are needed? Estimates vary, but research shows that each time a learner meets a new word in context, small gains are made in the understanding of meaning, grammar, spelling, and so on; after ten meetings in context, considerable learning has taken place. Ten encounters is considered a good "rule of thumb."[16] Even then, however, there may be gaps in the learner's understanding of the word.[17]

In fact, the number of repetitions is only one of the factors influencing learning. The spacing of intervals between the encounters and the types of tasks are also important. The rate at which we forget is fastest immediately after the word is presented; it then decreases with time. Therefore, be sure to repeat a new word soon after you first present it, and then at spaced intervals of increasing length.[18] Memorizing lists of words or cramming are not recommended by experts in memory.[19] The following suggestions may help you incorporate repetition of words into your classroom:

a. Recycling of target words will be easier if your target words are relevant and useful. Select words with this in mind.

b. Many encounters with new words are rich in information for the word learner, but are unnoticed as such, leading to what one researcher refers to as "unappreciated input."[20] Whenever possible, guide students toward noticing what is important.

c. Homework and classroom practice should provide repetition of words from both current and past lessons. Continue to provide practice with words after a unit is finished.

d. Keep a list of target words from past and present units in a visible place in the classroom (on a bulletin board or at the edge of the blackboard). Refer to the list often and try to use words in administrative tasks, (e.g., *Who will help me distribute the surveys?*), general classroom exchanges (e.g., *Were the instructions on the tests explicit enough?*), and reading discussions (e.g., *What do you think was the main incentive for the president's reaction?*).

e. Establish a "Word of the Week" program. At the beginning of the week, give each teacher in a program or school the same academic word. Have them write the word on the board or post it on a bulletin board in clear view. Ask the teachers to use the word naturally in class, as often as possible, throughout the week. They should simply use the words and comment on them based on their own knowledge. This kind of program will expose students to multiple meanings, collocations, connotations, and so on. You might also have students compare word uses from one class to another.

The importance of repetition to word learning is one thing that all vocabulary researchers agree on. Teachers need to regularly plan ways to practice words in class and not leave multiple exposures to chance.[21]

4 Provide Effective Vocabulary Practice

The explanations and definitions of words that you provide are not what learners need most, and too much explanation is confusing. What word learners really need is a teacher who facilitates relevant discussions and authentic opportunities to use target words.

Batia Laufer, a respected researcher of second language word learning, has studied, among other issues, the distinction between receptive word knowledge (the ability to recognize a word) and productive word knowledge (the ability to use it). Learners are often held back by limited productive vocabularies. In her Active Vocabulary Threshold Hypothesis, Laufer suggests that our receptive vocabularies develop throughout our lives, but that our "productive lexicon will grow only until it reaches the average level of the group in which we are required to function."[22] That is, if learners don't need certain words to interact in their environment, they may be able to recognize those words, but they probably will not be able to use them.

The following suggestions can help you provide effective practice of new words.

Structure your lessons carefully

Whenever possible, select topics about which students have considerable background information. Known information will help students predict, clarify, and position new information. It will also help learners recognize patterns and context clues. In addition, it's a good idea to stay within one content area for as long as it is interesting and relevant. Make use of familiar vocabulary and repeated themes. Such repetition helps students develop understanding of new words and leads them toward mastery of partially known words.

Use the words that you have introduced in class in your activities, and, whenever possible, sequence the practice from a focus on the word and its properties (word level), to the use of the word in sentences (sentence level), and eventually to free practice. Similar to the progression from controlled, semi-controlled, and free practice,[23] this allows learners first to focus on words in isolation and to gradually master the layers of knowledge needed for using the word in original expression.

Provide stimulating contexts

Use interesting and relevant contexts and make the most of them. Context, by definition, includes the situation in which something happens. Some contexts are naturally provided through reading or listening assignments. When context is not available or adequate for vocabulary practice, you can situate words by using pictures. Select target words with reference to a specific picture and have students use the words to describe the situation or tell a story about what might be happening. Other sources of context include hypothetical situations (e.g., *Imagine that you are writing a letter to…*), and games (e.g., PICTIONARY or charades). These are far more effective techniques than providing a list of words in isolation and having students write sentences.

Make practice meaningful, interactive, and focused

The most engaging activities create opportunities for learners to need the target words in order to express themselves. Include activities that have students practice such functions as describing, comparing, contrasting, ranking, summarizing, restating, and discussing. There are many suggestions for meaningful activities at the end of each chapter in this book, starting with Chapter 2.

Be alert to "teachable moments" when practice might fit into a place that is relevant but unexpected. This kind of unplanned discussion and practice can be very effective for learning. For example, during a discussion of an upcoming TOEFL exam, one teacher noticed that a target word *redress* appeared on the TOEFL registration form. She took advantage of the opportunity to talk about the meaning of the word and to point out the collocation *seek redress*. This was a perfect teachable moment because the information was highly relevant to the students as they nervously anticipated the test.

It takes time to reflect on word use, to learn to notice what's important, and to express oneself with new words. Learn to recognize when students are engaged in useful analysis or practice, and give them the time they need.

Facilitate student-centered group work. Circulate while students work, and listen to them carefully before responding. Model a positive attitude toward experimenting with the language—errors are often a sign of risk-taking. Help learners focus on the target words or structures of the class; if they are working with collocations, focus your correction on their use of collocations, not on uncountable nouns or articles. Guide students toward staying on task without monopolizing the discussions, even though they might seem to invite it. Remind them that this is their time for practice. Try not to draw attention away from the focus of the activity by going off on a tangent (e.g., *Oh, I've been to Rome, and I loved it. Have you seen…?*).

5 Monitor Your Students' Understanding

It's important to keep your finger on the pulse of what your students understand and what they don't. This isn't always easy. It requires that you get a lot of feedback from them through tests, quizzes, and discussions, but those aren't enough.

As you circulate while students are working in groups, listen carefully to their uses of target words. Get a feel for what they know and what they need to work on. Do they know that a particular verb is transitive or that another word is formal? Avoid jumping in to correct errors immediately, however. You want students to be as relaxed as possible.

Another feedback-gleaning technique can be done during the last five minutes of class: Ask students to take out a piece of scratch paper and do a quick task (see suggestions below)—not for a grade, but just for your information. Students needn't put their names on their work.

Sample Tasks

a. Write this sentence on the board: *Use ____ to describe _____.* Select a word that was covered in class and give students a context in which to use it. For example, have students use a form of the word *access* to describe the facilities for students on campus (e.g., *I like the computer labs, but they would be more accessible if they were open longer.* OR *When I tried to access help in the library, I had to wait a long time.*).

b. Write a list of five recently studied words on the board and have students rank them from 1 to 5 according to how likely they are to use them.

c. Have students rank a list of five words according to how difficult they are to pronounce.

d. Have students each select one word from the day's discussion that was new to them and that seems useful. Ask students to give a specific example of where they think they might use it.

e. Ask students if they have any questions about the words covered in the day's class (or about topics that were covered such as col-locations, countable nouns, etc.).

The format of this book is designed, first, to help you raise your own word consciousness, and then, to help you provide your students with information and practice. In each of Chapters 2–6, the focus is on one of the layers of word knowledge: meaning(s), colloca-tions, grammatical features, word parts, and register and other language variation. The beginning of each chapter provides back-ground to help you notice what is included in each layer. (For exam-ple, in Chapter 2, on meaning, the background section discusses multiple meanings, meaning boundaries, and connotations.) The main part of each chapter offers a closer look at that particular layer of word knowledge. The end of each chapter presents a selection of classroom activities. These activities offer practice at the word level. Many activities include a sentence-level follow-up, giving students the opportunity to use words in original sentences or in longer discourse. All of the activities draw attention to general principles that can be applied to lifelong word learning. Finally, Chapter 7 focuses on guiding students toward becoming independent word learners.

Working with Meaning

"… a New England horse-trader sold a farmer
a nag under the guarantee that she
was 'strong, and without fault.'
When on the way home, the farmer's new purchase
walked bang into a stone wall,
he turned back and protested furiously that the horse,
despite the warranty, was blind.
'Ah, sir,' replied the dealer, 'blindness is not her fault;
it's her misfortune.'"[1]

BACKGROUND

When we know a word, we know its "full meaning potential"[2]; this means many things. For the New England horse-trader in the anecdote above, it means that he knew the word *fault* had more than one meaning: the farmer interpreted "… without fault" as "without shortcomings," whereas the horse-trader claimed to interpret it as "without responsibility." We can see that the storyteller had a thorough knowledge of the meaning potential of the words he so carefully chose. He used *nag*, a word with a negative connotation ("old, worn-out") rather than *horse*. He achieved a comic tone with careful wording to describe the actions. The horse "walked bang into a stone wall" and the man "protested furiously." The images are vivid, and we can picture the events with ease. The skill of using multiple meanings of words, connotations, and subtleties of meaning with such agility is a powerful tool… and a very difficult one to acquire.

   To know the meaning of a word includes knowing what various word choices will accomplish. This requires knowing more than definitions; it includes understanding the subtle differences between words. For example, imagine that your boss has asked you to stay late at work. You want to make a good impression on her, but you have plans and you really don't want to change them. Word knowledge allows you the finesse to be honest but still somewhat vague, and to control (even manipulate) the impression that you make: e.g., *I'm sorry, I have an appointment / a meeting / an engagement / a prior commitment*. If your audience were different (a friend perhaps), you might choose to be more specific: e.g., *a manicure appointment / a blind date that your friends arranged for you / plans to test drive a car you want to buy*. As the examples show, word choice provides a lot of freedom of expression. By choosing different words, you can subtly suggest different things about the nature of an event, and you can influence how formal, official, or even legitimate it might seem to the listener. Making effective choices gives you control over how much information you divulge, how familiar you want to be with your audience, and the impression you want to make. Word choices allow you to be:

> vague or specific: We have plans. / We have a dinner date.

> formal or informal: We're attending a friend's party. / We're checking out Joe's bash.

> direct or indirect: Your paper was lousy. / Your paper needs work.

> candid or discreet: He's rich! / He has a comfortable income.

Precise word choices can also express subtle differences in meaning. For example:

> He requested / demanded my presence at the meeting.

> They talked / gossiped quietly in a corner.

> The government received / collected the fee.

> Their kitchen is clean / sanitary.

Again, we are reminded that word learning is an enormous task. When we strive to express ourselves, just look at the choices we have between words with similar meanings, and consider how much detailed information about each word we need in order to make these decisions. Teachers certainly cannot "teach" all that students need to know about meaning, so we should strive to set the stage for its discovery. We can help learners develop word consciousness so they can learn how to notice the information they need. We can provide them with practice and encourage them to seek further practice on their own; each observation or use of a target word is a chance to learn more about its meaning potential.

A CLOSER LOOK AT MEANING

Learning new word meanings in another language poses unique challenges. You can help learners by raising their awareness of how to go about the process of learning a word's meaning. This includes making the best use of definitions and background knowledge. It also includes the awareness that subtle features of word meaning can make or break the accurate use of a word.

1 Definitions and Word Learning

Definitions are an important part of word learning, but they are not sufficient.[3] A good learner examines a definition with the awareness that definitions are only a starting point; they don't provide all the information you need to use the word. The professor and vocabulary specialist, Margaret McKeown, tells a story about her own learning of the word *infatuate* at the age of twelve. She had read the definition, "to affect with folly," and interpreted it to mean "to joke around or make someone laugh." Her assignment was to prepare a sentence using the word.

> The boy I sat next to in class…always had something funny to say. So my sentence was, "I'm infatuated with Tim Gray." Luckily, before I had a chance to share my sentence with the class, the discussion of the word's meaning led me to realize that it basically meant to have a crush on someone. Whew![4]

The young McKeown started with the definition, applied it as it fit with her experience, then was wise enough to keep listening for more information about the word to confirm her understanding.

Definitions are usually brief and can be inadequate. For example, one dictionary definition of the word *streak* is "to run or move very fast." Based on so little information, it would be hard to create a good sentence. It would help the learner to read a couple of sample sentences or ask a few questions: Who or what might streak? Are there any connotations? Who might use this word? Without the benefit of information beyond the definition, one student wrote:

*When I am 60, I hope that I can streak like I do now.

Similarly, synonyms alone provide little information for the learner. Unless they are supplemented with sample sentences and additional information, misunderstandings can occur. For example, one dictionary states that *retrieve* and *recover* are synonyms. This led a student to write:

*She was in a coma, but she retrieved.

Research has shown that definitions are valuable in that they position a new word in relation to other words.[5] Definitions usually classify a word by placing it in a more general category, and then identifying details that distinguish it from other words in that category. The words *feeling* and *vegetable* are **classifiers** in the following sentences: *Anxiety is a feeling of worry or fear. A carrot is a long, thin, orange vegetable.* Learning a target word's relationship to more general and more specific words is a good starting place from which to gather more information. See Chapter 7 for further discussion and practice of classifiers and dictionary use.

2 Background Knowledge and Word Learning

The meaning that you assign to a new word is closely linked to what you already know. That is, the knowledge you have is a great asset as you learn new information. This might be as simple as noticing the words that are used in combination with a new word. For example, we can learn a lot about the word wimp ("a feeble, timid, or ineffectual person") by noticing familiar words that are used with it: *pale-faced wimp, pathetic wimps, wimps and cowards.*[6]

The association of words with personal experience is another way that familiar information facilitates the learning of new information. Word learning is more difficult when most of the information is new and devoid of associations, as is true of most lists.[7] For example, it is much more difficult to learn a list of different emotions (*happy, angry, sad, frustrated,* etc.) than it is to focus on one emotion at a time, and associate each one with some familiar experiences:

I am <u>frustrated</u> when I am running late, and I can't find my car keys. Or when my paycheck is late.

I feel <u>exhilarated</u> after I take a run. Or after a good conversation with an interesting person.

Similarly, it is harder to learn the months of the year in a list than it is to learn one month at a time, and relate each one to familiar information:

December is my favorite month. I like the cold weather because I can wear hats and drink hot soup by the fire. I also like to go skiing and ice skating.

A person's background experience certainly includes his or her first language. Words almost never transfer exactly from one language to another. For example, in Greek, γεια σου (/ya su/) can mean both *hello* and *goodbye*. In Spanish, the word *derecha* can mean the direction "right" or "straight," depending on the gender of the addressee and the grammatical structure of the sentence. When you say "siga derecha" you are talking to a female and telling her to go straight. "Siga a la derecha" means "turn right" for anybody, regardless of gender. Some differences are obscure; it often takes time and careful attention to uncover the details of the meaning differences among words.

3 The Details of a Word's Meaning

Meaning boundaries

Linguists acknowledge that the boundaries between words can be unclear or "fuzzy."[8] For example, the word *furniture* is defined as "the moveable items required for use or ornament in a house, office, etc." This would include chairs, tables, cabinets, and bookcases. But it's difficult to pinpoint the (mysterious) boundary that would keep us from using the word *furniture* for toasters, stereo speakers, and paintings. Such boundaries vary across languages and dialects, causing considerable confusion for the learner.

Word boundaries pose another type of problem when learners translate from their first language. The meanings of a word and its translation may seem the same at first, but the boundaries of the words make them slightly different. For example, in Spanish, *niños* means children, and only refers to young children. Thus, it is quite understandable how a Spanish speaker made the following error in English:

*I don't have any children; they are all grown up now.

Such differences in word boundaries exist among all languages. For example, in Greek, μπλε (/ble/) refers to all shades of blue except sky blue, and πόδι (/boδi/) refers to the leg and the foot together. In Japanese, the fish we know as a striped mullet has several names, depending on its size: *haku* (about 3 cm); *subashiri* or *oboko* (about 5–10 cm), *ina* (about 20 cm), *bora* (about 30–40 cm), and *todo* (about 50 cm or larger). The effective learner will look at the basic translation of a new word and then watch for both similarities and differences in meaning between the two languages.

Meaning domains

A **meaning domain** refers to the limits on the environments in which a word can be used. For example, some words are only used in reference to males; others are only used with reference to females. We would not say:

> *The woman was portly.
> *The man was very pretty.

Other usages are determined by animacy (a category including animals and humans). That is, some words are used only in reference to humans, some words, only in reference to animals, and others only in reference to inanimate objects. For example, we would not say:

> *She went to the manicurist because her talon was broken.
> *The entity standing over there is my sister.
> *They have an adorable baby thing.
> *My mechanic told me the car was incurable.
> *The green objects in the salad were delicious.

Distinctions such as these are influenced by culture and can vary greatly across languages, quite noticeably in reference to animals. For example, in English we can refer to a dog as a "girl dog" or a "boy dog," and we readily say "Good boy" or "Good girl." However, in Spanish one would never refer to dogs with the words used for human girls and boys (*chica* / *chico* or *niña* / *niño*). A female dog is *perra* and a male dog is *perro*. This difference occurs in many languages. In Urdu, a female dog is "kutti" and a male is "kutta," and they would never be referred to by the human equivalents.

Word form and word meaning

There are some word forms that can be deceptive. Sometimes the form of an unfamiliar word makes it look like a word that the learner already knows. In that case, the learner won't even realize that the word is indeed a new word.[9] There are several ways that words can seem familiar when they are not.

Synforms are words that look or sound like another word in the target language (*acute / cute, legible / eligible, cautious / conscious*, etc.). Such confusion between words is very problematic for readers.[10] Synforms are also a problem for writers:

*I had jet lack.
*I am sorry to interpret your class.
*Thank you for your corporation.
*The buzzard went off at the end of the game.
*We bought beer at the liquid store.
*I value the importants of my culture.

False friends are words in the second language (L2) that look or sound like words in the first language (L1). Learners assume they are the same, but the meanings are quite different.

ENGLISH WORD	L1 WORD	L1 TRANSLATION
cynic	tsinik (Bulgariah)	vulgar, low class person
molest	molestar (Spanish)	to bother
enjoy	enjoyer (Spanish)	to adorn with jewels
berate	beraten (German)	advise, discuss
lust	Lust (German) lust (Swedish)	wish, intent
casino	casino (Italian)	brothel
coffin	couffin (French)	baby basket
full	full (Swedish & Norwegian)	drunk or inebriated

Errors with morphology occur when students know the parts of words but put them together incorrectly. This occurs when they think that every word part is meaningful. For example, a learner might interpret *outline* to mean "out of the line." Similarly, problems occur when learners create their own words or definitions, based on their own literal interpretation of the parts.

WORD	LEARNER'S DEFINITION
submarine	a marine who is under water
terminal illness	a computer that is out of order
*sunshower	sitting in the sun as it showers down upon you (sunbath)

See Chapter 5 for further discussion of word parts.

4 Connotation and Shades of Meaning

Connotations, or nuances, are ideas suggested by a word in addition to its main meaning. They are critical to everyday language use because they can evoke very different positive or negative ideas or associations. For example, a sentence can be changed from polite to rude with slight variation:

> He is careful / timid / afraid of his shadow.

> The lady was interested / inquisitive / a snoop.

> She is a social drinker / overindulging / a lush.[11]

Consider the plight of the language learner who is trying to describe a person whose body type is smaller than the norm. The connotations of the following words range from complimentary to insulting:

> slender, slight, lean, slim, thin, delicate, lanky, skinny, scrawny, underweight, lean, emaciated

This is also true for descriptions of a person whose body type is the opposite:

> sturdy, solid, burly (for men only), stocky, plump, fleshy, overweight, stout, pudgy, chubby, fat

Connotation is a powerful tool that can be used to express a variety of perspectives and values. For example, to show discretion in Victorian times, people referred to the legs (of tables) as *limbs* and underwear as *unmentionables*. Today, it is more respectful to use *senior citizens* rather than *old people* and *impoverished* or *poor area* rather than *slum*. Such usages are considered **euphemisms** when they are seen as an attempt to hide something embarrassing or unpleasant (See Chapter 6 for further discussion of euphemisms). For example, businesspeople say that a company has *downsized* instead of *fired employees*. Learning the connotations of words is both important and challenging for the language learner because they are, by nature, intertwined with the L2 culture. That is, they lessen the directness or unpleasantness of a concept, thus reflecting the values and fears of a certain group.

5 Multiple Meanings

Many words in English have multiple meanings, which makes them very difficult for learners. They encounter a word they think they know, and in fact it has a whole new meaning. So in addition to the challenge presented by new words, learners also face the challenge of "known" words.

Words that have more than one meaning are often referred to as polysemous words. For our purposes, we will focus on **homonyms**, words that have the same form but different meanings, such as *bug* ("an insect", "a technical device", "or an illness"), *state* ("a province or a situation"), and *bank* ("the edge of a river" or "a place for your money").

The word *since* is another example. It means "from the time when" or "because," implying different meanings for the following sentences:

The government became rich since it took money from the poor.

Since Meg started her own business, she became rich.

Homonyms can be problematic for both the reader and the writer because learners often assume that the familiar meaning is the only meaning; they can be reluctant to abandon a familiar meaning, even when it doesn't make sense.

KEY CONSIDERATIONS FOR THE CLASSROOM

Meanings can't be taught; learners discover meaning through language use and observation. Teachers can help by giving brief and accurate definitions, and then by providing ample opportunity for discovery through practice. Many of the details of meaning are acquired through exposure to rich and expressive language from a variety of sources.[12] As discussed in Chapter 1, instruction and practice that is spaced throughout several lessons is more effective than an intense amount of information delivered at one time; learners are capable of taking in just so much at a time.[13]

1 Dealing with Definitions

Provide effective definitions

The teacher who can briefly and clearly capture the heart of a new word is a word learner's best friend. If you develop this skill, you will find that you call upon it nearly every day in the classroom. Follow these general guidelines when you define words:

a. Use everyday language.

b. Focus on the central or basic meaning, and then move on to the subtleties.

c. Include at least one sample sentence. Sample sentences can help you as much as they help the student because they enable you to remember the most important details of meaning.

d. Focus on the meaning-of-the-moment. That is, focus on the meaning of a word in the context you are working with. However tempting it may be, don't try to cover all of the meanings of the word at once. Allow the information in the context to guide you. If a student asks about a word used outside of class, find out what the context was (Ask, "Where did you hear / see the word?").

Learn to use different approaches for explaining different words. Always remember to keep your explanation concise, and follow it up by choosing among the many available ways to elucidate a word's meaning:

■ examples

■ negative examples (*"Sprint* is like *run,* but it's faster and shorter."*)*

■ synonyms

■ antonyms

■ situational contexts (*He felt <u>jealous</u> when his wife talked to other men.*)

■ realia (food items, tools, and other materials)

■ gesture

■ pantomime or demonstration

Have students practice new words in class so that you can hear their sentences and see if their understanding is clear and complete. Learners may respond to definitions differently from what you expect. Errors, such as those in the sentences below, can result from a lack of clarity on the part of the teacher or from a misunderstanding of the definition by the student. In any case, it is easy to clarify the confusion if you hear the learners' sentences.

inhabitant: a person or animal that lives in a place

*The inhabitants of the car were unhurt in the accident.

decade: a period of ten years

*I rode the bus for decades of hours.

Help learners use dictionaries effectively

Dictionaries are underused by many learners. It is a worthwhile investment of class time to model and practice a variety of dictionary skills. For example, during a class discussion, stop and look up a word that is unfamiliar to many students. Model the process of (1) interpreting the abbreviations and notes (for parts of speech, formality, verb completions, etc.); (2) using an alphabetical list; (3) removing the inflection if the word is inflected; (4) using the context to decide which meaning to select. See Chapter 7 for further discussion of dictionary use.

2 Help Learners Talk about Meaning

Learners benefit when they ask the right questions about a new word. You can help by making your students aware of the information they may need:

- Does the word have any synonyms? Does it have any antonyms?

- What other words could be used here instead of this one?

- Is the word being used literally or figuratively?

- Could the word be used to refer to people? Animals? Things?

- Does the word have any positive or negative connotations?

It is also important for learners to seek clarification about words. Demonstrate the kinds of questions they might ask:

"Is this word similar to ___?"

"Do you mean ____?"

"How is this word different from ____?"

Encourage your students to ask questions, and be supportive. Remember that questions can be good indications of the development of word consciousness. Some questions will be harder to answer. Be sure to acknowledge those questions as good questions that will need some thought. Since much of your word knowledge is intuitive, you might need to research a question or ask other proficient speakers. Find the answers, and follow up in the next class.

As you model and practice the navigation of meaning with good questions about meaning and helpful answers, you are providing independent word learning tools that students will emulate long after your class is over.

3 Beware of the Learning Burden Posed by Meaning

In Chapter 1 we saw that some words are more difficult to learn than others. With respect to meaning, the learning burden is heavier for words that are abstract than for those that are concrete. It is also more difficult to learn a word when it has connotations that don't exist in the first language. In addition, a word is more difficult if it has multiple meanings or false friends.

ACTIVITIES

1 Word Ranking and Reshuffling

Goal: Learners use categorization and ranking to examine the meanings of target words.

Procedure:

1. Select 5–8 target words that you can identify as belonging to one of the categories below, or create your own categories.

2. Determine criteria for ranking the target words.

3. Students work in pairs to rank the words according to the appropriate criteria (1 = the most, 3–4 = the least). Pairs then compare rankings with other pairs before coming together for a class discussion to explain their rationale. Explain to students that the answers will vary.

CATEGORIES AND WORDS	CRITERIA				
Personal Qualities	**Importance for work**	**Importance for personal relationships**	**Importance for travel**	**Importance for a better world**	**General frequency of word**
assertiveness	*1*				
patience	*2*				
frugality	*3*				

	Technological Advances/ Machines	Affordability	Practicality	Dependability	Entertainment value	Importance to people, in general
MRI	*1*					
DVD player	*3*					
Global positioning systems (GPS)	*2*					

	Reading Materials	Popularity	Educational value	Entertainment value	Timelessness	Importance for our culture, in general
newspaper				*2*		
magazines				*3*		
novels				*1*		
textbooks				*4*		

2 Reflecting on Meaning[14]

Goal: Learners examine the meaning of a few target words and consider various ways that they can be used.

Procedure:

1. Create a chart similar to the sample below. List 5–8 target words, along with sample sentences and questions for each one. Divide students into pairs, and give each pair a copy of the chart. Review the chart with the class.

2. Students work in pairs to answer the questions for one target word at a time. After the pairs have had enough time to discuss two or three words, stop for a class discussion to check for comprehension and appropriate usage.

3. Pairs then continue to answer the questions about the remaining words.

4. Pairs exchange charts with other pairs and review the results. Finally, hold a class discussion that focuses on the variety of possible usages and the specific meaning characteristics of each word.

DEFINITION AND SAMPLE SENTENCE	QUESTIONS
1. release: to set something free *The prisoner was released after she completed her sentence.*	a. What are five things that can be released? b. What is wrong with the following sentence? *He released when he got home from work.*
2. saturate: to make something very wet or to fill completely *She spilled her coffee on her notebook, and it was saturated.*	a. What are five things that might be saturated by a heavy rain? b. Explain this sentence: *The market was saturated by inexpensive computers.* c. What do you think a saturated market is? d. What are some things that you think saturate the market now?

3 Practice with Multiple Meanings[15]

Goal: Learners identify the multiple meanings of several words and decide which meanings are more basic than others.

Procedure:

1. Write the following list of words on the board. Students work in pairs to list as many meanings as possible for each word.

head	page	foot	ring
pack	bill	bank	

2. In pairs, students decide whether any of the meanings seem more

central or basic, and mark them accordingly in preparation for a class discussion.

3. Lead a class discussion about the students' findings, drawing attention to meanings that are literal versus figurative and frequent versus infrequent.

Sentence-level follow-up:

Review the meaning of the word *nonsense* with the class. Then have students work in pairs to write a nonsense sentence that uses as many of the words from the list as possible. Go over the examples, pointing out how it uses multiple meanings of the words.

> **Example**
>
> The page was headed for the bank of the river with his head held high and a ring in his pack before he turned the page of his contract and realized that he would have to foot the bill for the ring, so he quickly turned back and went to City Bank.

4 Human or Not? Part A

Goal: Learners categorize words according to what they can refer to: people, animals, objects, or a combination.

Procedure:

1. Write the sample chart on the board (see below), and review the categories with the class.

2. Show students how to categorize and code the target words according to how they are used:

   √ = This word is used to refer to this category.

   X = This word cannot be used to refer to this category.

   ? = I'm not sure whether this word can refer to this category.

3. Students complete the chart, and then compare answers with the class.

4. In pairs or small groups, students add their own target words to the chart and categorize them.

TARGET WORDS	PEOPLE	ANIMALS (If you choose this column, give an example)	THINGS (If you choose this column, give an example)
Nouns			
man/woman	✓	x	x
male/female	✓	all animals	some plants
species			
medley			
Verbs			
garnish (to decorate)			
breed			
cultivate			
produce			
train			
decorate			
Adjectives			
refined			
traditional			
kind			
harsh			
eternal			
domesticated			
conservative			

Sentence-level follow-up:

1. Point out that the meanings of words sometimes change when they are used in reference to people, animals, or things. Have students consider the meanings of the words in the following phrases.
   a. harsh woman / harsh winter
   b. traditional parents / traditional wedding
   c. refined sugar / refined person

2. Students write a sentence for each phrase, using a dictionary as needed. They should be prepared to discuss how meaning can shift when the same word is used in different categories.

3. Point out that some words are normally used with animals, but they can be used in reference to people to make a humorous or special point. For example:
   a. to breed children
   b. a domesticated husband

4. Ask students what effect the writer of the two phrases above might be trying to create. Have them write sentences using each phrase. Lead a class discussion about how meaning can shift when the same word is used in different categories.

5 Human or Not? Part B[16]

Goal: Learners identify words that can be used in reference to people, animals, things, and combinations thereof.

Procedure:

1. Write three columns on the board, and label them: People, Animals, Both.

2. Elicit examples for each category, explaining to students that these distinctions may be different in other languages. Encourage examples from all parts of speech. Review pages 19–20 of this chapter, if needed.

3. Students work in pairs to list 5–10 words for each category.

4. Lead a class discussion about the results. Focus on the differences that occur across languages and the cultural attitudes that are

reflected in these usages. Notice that, in English, there are many words that are used for both animals and people.

6 Meanings with "Shades" and Connotations

Goal: Learners recognize the variation that is possible in selecting words with different shades of meaning and connotations, and they identify the settings in which different choices would be effective.

Procedure:

1. List on the board about five neutral adjectives to describe people (e.g., *tall, short, large, small, quiet,* etc.).

2. Students work in pairs to identify positive and negative examples of each word [e.g., *tall: statuesque* (positive); *gawky* (negative)]. Encourage students to use a thesaurus and to check the meanings in a dictionary as needed.

3. In a class discussion, have students compare their findings, focusing on the settings in which each word might be used. Not every connotation will be interpreted in the same way; encourage discovery as students compare observations.

7 How STRONG are these words?

Goal: Learners identify the relative strength of related words, and choose from the range of meanings to express themselves.

Procedure:

1. On the board, list about five adjective pairs with similar meanings; one word in the pair should be weak and the other strong (e.g., *displeased / incensed; competent / expert; pleased / elated; unpleasant / dreadful; remove / annihilate*).

2. For each word pair, draw a straight line on the board to represent a continuum of word strength, with the weak word on the left, the strong on the right, and space for additional words in between. If you have enough space, draw a line long enough to allow several students to work at the board at the same time.

3. Working in pairs, students copy the continuums on their own paper. They add 3–4 words to each continuum, positioning the

words according to their relative strength. Encourage students to use a thesaurus and to check meanings in a dictionary as needed. A thesaurus is available in Microsoft Word for help. For example:

displeased   unhappy   angry   exasperated   incensed

<--->

4. Have students come to the board and add their words to each continuum, placing them in relation to the other words that have been added already. Answers may not be clear-cut, so encourage students to experiment.

5. Follow-up: Use target words that have been studied in class. Identify similar words that are stronger and weaker, and arrange them on continuums, as above.

Sentence-level follow-up:

Explain the following scenario and task to the class:

To prepare for this assignment, select a job that you would like to have. Pretend that you have applied for this job, and that you have asked your professor to write a letter of reference. Now, imagine that you are your professor. Write a brief letter, recommending you for the job. Use as many of the words from the word-strength chart as possible. OR: Write a letter that you hope your professor would NOT write on your behalf. (Be sure to include the name of the job in your letter.)

8 Where are the boundaries?[17]

Goal: Learners examine words that belong to a category and identify what those words have in common.

Procedure:

1. Write three columns on the board, following the model below.

2. First, clarify the games listed in column 1. Then, divide students into small groups, and have groups add more examples of games to the chart.

3. Each group works together to create a definition of the word *game*. To guide students, ask: What do these examples of games have in common? Groups share their definitions with the class. If time

allows, have students compare their answers with dictionary definitions and comment on which of their definitions best captured the meanings.

4. Have the class continue working with the other categories in the chart. Provide examples for your students, or let them generate their own.

GAMES	CAREERS	VEGETABLES
chess Olympic Games baseball hopscotch poker tennis solitaire handball backgammon soccer		

9 Learning Words That Belong Together[18]

Goal: Learners examine the meanings of partially known words for the purpose of relating them to one another and using them in original sentences.

Procedure:

1. Select about ten recently studied words. Write them on the board and review the meanings as needed.

2. Working in pairs, students pick two words and explain how they might relate to each other. For example, if *gregarious* and *eavesdropping* were chosen, an explanation could be, "It's easy to eavesdrop on gregarious people." Allow enough time for students to select several word pairs and several explanations for them.

3. In a class discussion, compare similarities and differences in how words were used.

10 Predicting Main Ideas

Goal: Learners focus on target words to predict the main ideas of an article based on a variety of textual clues such as titles, subtitles, pictures, and captions.

Procedure:

1. Select a picture associated with an article / story that the students will read. In some textbooks, an appropriate picture will appear with the article. In other cases, you can find a picture in other printed material or on the Internet.

2. Select 5–10 target words from the Academic Word List (AWL) that will guide students toward the central meaning of the article. The AWL can be found online at http://language.massey.ac.nz/staff/awl/.

3. Briefly review the meanings of the target words and preview all textual clues available in the article (titles, subtitles, pictures, captions, etc.).

4. Before reading, students work in pairs to use the target words in sentences that express their predictions about the main ideas of the article. Circulate among the groups to help students use different forms of the target words effectively.

Sentence-level follow-up:

After reading the article, students write a short paragraph summarizing the article and commenting on the accuracy of their predictions (e.g., "I thought this article was going to be critical of plastic surgery, but in fact it was quite positive."). Encourage students to use appropriate forms of the target words in their paragraphs.

Working with Collocation

CHAPTER 3

Lonely word seeks like-minded partners for possible collocation. Single, English, connotation doesn't matter. Enjoy participating in long chunks, multi-word phrases and phrasal verbs. (Euphemisms need not apply.)

BACKGROUND

Knowing a word includes knowing the company it keeps. That is, words do not always act as isolated units, and we must recognize the ways they co-occur. For example, we would say *tall man* (not *high man*), *numbers of people* (not *sums of people*) and *last but not least* (rather than *least but not last*). **Collocation** refers to the ways words are combined with each other. Collocation has been called "a marriage contract between words," with the caveat that "some words are more firmly married than others."[1]

Collocations exist in every known language. They are evident in the speech of very young children, and they are an important part of the semantic network building in the minds of language users.[2] The proficient speaker isn't usually conscious of the principle of collocation until it is violated. For example, we might not realize that *step* collocates with *take*, but we would recognize that something is wrong with this sentence:

> *If a couple is not happy together, marriage was probably the wrong step for them to do.

Similarly, a teacher may present a single target word, such as *volcano* or *tire*, and not realize the need to point out their collocations until a learner produces sentences such as these:

> *The volcano isn't working.
> *My tire broke on the freeway.

We might also not be aware that some words occur in a consistent order, until we see combinations such as these:

*forth and back	*tall, handsome, and dark
*groom and bride	*look low and high
*night, noon, and morning	*death and life
*stripes and stars	*sour and sweet sauce
*a matter of death or life	*swim or sink

Words clearly do not work alone. Like people, words tend to change greatly when put with various "partners." For example, consider how the meaning of *hard* changes when combined with different nouns; this becomes clear when you consider the opposites.

COLLOCATES OF *HARD*	OPPOSITES
hard exam	easy exam
hard chair	soft or comfortable chair
hard work	effortless work
hard-nosed person	lenient or easygoing person

In addition, when we are "reaching for a word," we need to know more than its meaning. We also need to know how it combines with other words. For example, we can use *large* to describe some nouns, but not others.

WE CAN SAY...	BUT NOT...
large problem	*large solution
large family	*large attitude
large amount	*large advice
large part	*large discrimination
large room	*large significance

Some language forms follow fairly predictable rules. For example, to form the simple past of a regular verb, add an *-ed* ending. Collocations are different; they generally do not follow many rules, and they are hard to predict. The main rule is that words do co-occur, and we need to be observant about how they do it. As teachers, our job is first to be alert to collocation. Then we need to teach learners to notice collocation and to recognize it as an important part of using words well. The process begins with raising students' word consciousness and continues with providing interactive classroom practice that draws attention to the principle of collocation at work.

A CLOSER LOOK AT COLLOCATION

1 The Principle of Collocation

As we have seen, words do not function as isolated units. One type of collocation occurs in the choice of certain adjective–noun combinations.

WE SAY...	BUT NOT...
big (or fat) stomach	*thick stomach
thick waisted	*thick stomached
wide-eyed	*broad-eyed
long legs	*lengthy legs

Similarly, collocations occur with many verb–noun pairs.

WE SAY...	BUT NOT...
prices rose	*prices levitated
the pain disappeared	*the pain recovered
do homework	*make homework
take a break	*do a break
make an effort	*take an effort

Most collocations are very hard to predict. Therefore, a target word's collocates are best learned along with the word itself, and they should be part of every discussion about a new word. For example, when the word *dismal* is taught, it makes sense to introduce words that often keep it company (*weather, day, prospects, future*) and words that do not (*method, clock*). Similarly, if a student had learned that the word *suicide* collocates with *commit*, he might have avoided writing this sentence:

> *He suicided in 1938.

Sometimes words are combined according to patterns. These patterns may help us predict some collocations. Three such patterns are discussed below. They can serve as a handy guideline, but are by no means foolproof.

Metaphor-based collocations

A **metaphor** is a way to talk about one thing in terms of another. For example, the literal meaning of *head* is the top part of the body; we also use this word to refer to the *head of a committee, the head of the line,* etc. Similarly, the literal *face of a person* can be extended to refer to the *face of a clock* or the *face of a mountain*. English uses many metaphors,[3] and sometimes they can help us learn how to collocate words.

For example, in English we talk about *time* as *money*. Both time and money are considered assets that we think and talk about in similar ways.

TIME IS MONEY	
Literal Use	**Metaphorical Use**
spend money	spend time
waste money	waste time
save money	save time
value money	value time
invest money	invest time

On the basis of this metaphor, it is possible to predict that you can use other "money verbs" with *time*. For example, you can also *steal time, count time, give time,* and *win time*.

There are many other metaphors that suggest that, as in many cultures, we tend to see one thing as similar to another.

ARGUMENTS ARE WAR	
Literal Use	**Metaphorical Use**
Wars break out.	Arguments break out.
Wars are waged.	Arguments are waged.
Wars are won / lost.	Arguments are won / lost.
Wars are provoked.	Arguments are provoked.

IDEAS ARE FASHIONS	
Literal Use	**Metaphorical Use**
Fashions are in vogue.	Ideas are in vogue.
Fashions are out of style.	Ideas are out of style.
Fashions are old hat.	Ideas are old hat.
Fashions are cutting edge.	Ideas are cutting edge.
Fashions are ahead of their time.	Ideas are ahead of their time.

POLITICS ARE SPORTS	
Literal Use	**Metaphorical Use**
An athlete runs a race.	A politician runs a race.
The athlete conceded defeat.	The politician conceded defeat.
An athlete scores points.	A politician scores points.
The runner won / lost the race.	The candidate won / lost the race.

Connotation-based collocations

Another pattern that may help us predict some collocations is the use of positive and negative connotations. That is, some words usually combine with positive words (*slight advantage*, not **slight crime*), and some words usually combine with negative words (*provoke trouble*, not **provoke fun*). Two good examples of this are *provide* and *cause*. *Provide* tends to collocate with positive words.

YOU CAN SAY...	BUT NOT...
provide care	*provide harm
provide money	*provide trouble or *provide poverty
provide food	*provide hunger
provide knowledge	*provide ignorance

Cause tends to collocate with negative words.

YOU CAN SAY	BUT NOT...
cause problems	*cause solutions
cause death	*cause life
cause war	*cause peace
cause an accident	*cause a safe trip
cause a divorce	*cause a marriage

Patterns such as these can be helpful, but they should be followed with caution. For example, you may hear combinations of cause with a positive word (e.g., *The circus clowns caused great pleasure among the children in the hospital.*).

Animacy-based collocations
A third pattern that can help predict appropriate collocations relates to human, or animate, characteristics. That is, we often use human words to relate to inhuman objects (e.g., *give birth to an idea; nurture a garden; feed a fire; nurse a drink*). This pattern does not always hold true, however, and can lead to errors:

*The truck was incurable.

*My car is blonde.

2 Types of Multi-Word Units

A collocation can function as a single word, a phrase, or a sentence. It is important for learners to be able to recognize these various forms.

Compound words

Sometimes words are used together so often that they become connected in our minds, and they function as a single word (e.g., *nuclear family, cosmetic surgery, space shuttle*). When pairs of words have been associated with each other for a long time, they become compound words. Sometimes these are written as single words (e.g., *bookcase, hardware, daycare, motorcyclist*), sometimes as hyphenated words (e.g., *dry-clean, brother-in-law, vice-president, first-degree*), and sometimes as two words (e.g., *DVD player, garden hose, fountain pen*). Over time, compounds tend to become written as single words, but the way they are written does not affect their use; they all operate as one-word units and are a very frequent type of collocation.[4]

Phrasal verbs

Phrasal verbs are usually made up of a one-syllable verb followed by a preposition (e.g., *turn on, build up, break off, put in*). Their meanings are sometimes transparent from the meaning of their parts (e.g., *give away, clean out, cheer up, tone down*), but other times this is not the case (e.g., *give in, call off, carry on, catch up*). Some phrasal verbs have corresponding noun forms, which are written as one word (e.g., a *buildup* of dirt or a dead *giveaway*). Phrasal verbs are so frequent in English that there are some dictionaries dedicated to them alone.

Lexical phrases

Lexical phrases are chunks of words or phrases that are "socially sanctioned independent units."[5] That is, each phrase is understood as a unit with a purpose. For example, *What on earth?* expresses surprise, *in a nutshell* is a summarizer, and "*Have you heard the one about…*" is used to introduce a joke. Lexical phrases are central to language use[6]; in fact, it has been claimed that they outnumber single words by ten to one.[7]

Idioms

An **idiom** is a lexical item in which the meaning of the whole is not immediately transparent from its parts. Idioms demonstrate that real language is far less literal than many of us think. Some commonly used idioms are *tongue-in-cheek, green thumb, thin-skinned, two left feet, frog in the throat*, and *knee-jerk reaction*.

Idioms are very important because they are a rich and frequent part of authentic language use. Sometimes idioms are fixed—the word order and word forms cannot be changed.

FIXED IDIOMS	
We can say . . .	**but not...**
kick the bucket	*punt the pail *or* *kick the nasty bucket
ear to the ground	*ear to the floor *or* *ear on the ground
bite the dust	*nibble the dirt
I'm all ears	*I'm partly ears.
raining cats and dogs	*raining dogs and cats *or* *snowing cats and dogs
curry favor	*curry approval

Other idioms allow more variation.

VARIABLE IDIOMS	
We can say...	**and...**
from head to foot	from head to toe
on the edge	on the brink / verge
up to my neck	up to my ears / eyeballs
not a prayer	not a hope / chance
cost an arm and a leg	pay an arm and a leg
air your dirty laundry	air your dirty linen

Idioms also tend to be very appealing to language learners. They're fun, and mastering them can help learners feel more connected to English speakers and their culture. As our word consciousness grows, we recognize that idioms are an intrinsic, not exceptional, part of language use, both at formal and conversational levels.

3 The Strength and Weakness of a Collocation

Collocational relationships vary from weak to strong. The strongest collocations are limited to a select number of words. For example, *blonde* occurs only with *hair* or *hair*-related words (e.g., *blonde wig, blonde curls*) and with *people* (e.g., *blonde beauty, blonde child*), but not with *chickens, carpets,* or *cars*. Other strong collocates are often associated with a particular word, though they might also occur in other combinations. For example, *identical* collocates strongly with *twins*, but it can also be paired with *dresses, problems, copies,* and *more*.

When words occur rather randomly with many other words, they are referred to as weak collocates (e.g., *nice, cheap, expensive, good, bad*). There are also words that combine in a more limited way than random pairings, but they are not as constrained as strong collocates. These might be considered collocates of medium strength (e.g., *carry out a study; conduct a study, do a study*). When learners understand the strength of a collocation, they are in a better position to judge when they can experiment with new combinations of words. This might help them avoid unacceptable sentences:

> *I had a broken tire on the freeway.
> *She will take an effort to improve.

It is important for language learners to be aware of the way words work together. As is true of other kinds of partnerships, some collocations are strong and binding; others are more flexible. These relationships between words are not easy to teach or to learn.[8] Such word knowledge is best acquired through an increased awareness of collocations, rich exposure to language in use, and ample opportunities for practice.

KEY CONSIDERATIONS FOR THE CLASSROOM

1 Pre-teach Collocations

Whenever possible, introduce new collocations as an integral part of pre-teaching a word or otherwise explaining meaning. We should always be thinking ahead about what our students will need when they start to actually use a new word. For example, if you introduce the word *economy*, mention some of its collocates: *global, healthy, depressed, stable, to build, to manage, to regulate.* If you teach the word *suicide*, remind students that it is a noun and that its verb collocate is *commit.*

Of course, we need to be selective in what we choose to pre-teach, due to time limitations and also because learners will be confused by too much information. Try to provide enough information to raise students' awareness of a new word's collocates and to help them create a few accurate sentences. After a very basic introduction to the new word, teachers need to provide opportunities for meaningful, interactive practice. Be sure to monitor students unobtrusively as they interact. Encourage them to experiment and to notice the important role of collocations in their language use.

2 Model the Process of Noticing Collocations

Your students will benefit from observing how you go about identifying collocations. It is good for them to see that this process takes careful reading and listening. For example, you might choose a short text to work on with the class. Select one noun that is of central importance, and then demonstrate the process of identifying and highlighting the verbs, adjectives, and adverbs that collocate with that noun. Learners can practice this process individually or in pairs, and then participate in a class discussion about their findings.

3 Raise Awareness of Language Transfer

All languages have collocations. It is common for learners to use collocations from their first language. For example, a German speaker might say *"write a test,"* or *"forth and back"*, based on the German collocations *"einen Test schreiben"* and *"him und her."* Learners may not realize that their home languages also contain collocations, but you can raise their awareness by sharing examples in class. Ask students from various first language backgrounds how they would translate phrases such as the following:

do homework	write a check
make headway	take after your mother
take an opportunity	pay attention
put on your coat	turn off the light
take off your coat	back the car up

A discussion like this can show learners that many collocations do not transfer from one language to another. It can also reinforce the point that words do not operate alone in any language, and that we learn the most about words when we study them in the "chunks" in which they naturally occur.

4 Learn Where to Get Information about Collocations

When asked directly, proficient speakers will be a good source of information about how to combine certain words in a phrase. For example:

> Question: Do I say "Please close the light"?
> Answer: No. You should say "Turn off the light."

But it is quite likely that they won't know the reason for the answer. For more complete information about collocation, there are some excellent sources that both teachers and learners can access easily.

Learner dictionaries: Dictionaries that are designed for English language learners often give collocates along with definitions. For example, in the *Oxford Advanced Learner's Dictionary*, the entry for *discriminate* has different definitions for *discriminate between* and *discriminate against*. Most general-use dictionaries provide as many as five definitions for *discriminate*, but they often don't mention collocations or how *discriminate between* differs in meaning from *discriminate against*.

Online concordancers: Concordancers offer large lists of authentic sentences (called concordance lines) that are gathered together from a corpus (plural: corpora). They are an excellent resource for the teacher or the learner who is investigating collocation. Concordancers are available as software packages and are sometimes offered online. They enable the user to look at a collection of sentences that all use the same word and to identify patterns. Below is a short excerpt from a concordancer.[9] Using a resource like this (but a much longer collection of sentences), you could ask a student to focus on the word *category*. Guiding questions, such as "What preposition is often used after this word?" and "What adjectives are used to describe this word?" can help the learner discover important collocational patterns.

14	rs, it would seem to fall into the	category	of chamber music- yet it calls for
15	government exist, we find a second	category	of countries with a different set
16	inal marriages still belong in the	category	of permissive unions; and core-Neg
17	s, that boats comprise the largest	category	of tangible personal property whic
18	alled his "Non-Dissonant (Mostly)"	category	of works. The Schuman "Chester" ta
19	forces, and area defense. The last	category	overlaps the others in amphibious
20	. Most countries in this second	category	share the difficulty of having man

You can find concordance lines such as these online by using the search term "online concordancers". Here are some examples:

Cobb, Tom. *The Compleat Lexical Tutor*. 2006. http://www.lextutor.ca (accessed October 2007).

Greaves, Chris. *Web Concordancer*. 1998. http://www.edict.com.hk/concordance/default.htm (accessed October 2007).

Haywood, Sandra. University of Nottingham website for academic vocabulary study. 2003. http://www.nottingham.ac.uk/~alzsh3/acvocab/ (accessed October 2007).

ACTIVITIES

1 Collocation Opposites[10]

Goal: Learners identify the opposites of target words and form correct collocations.

Procedure:

1. Choose a set of adjectives that have been covered in class. Examples of adjectives that would be good for this activity include *hard, soft, light, simple, general, low,* and *rough* because they can collocate with a variety of nouns.

2. Write a three-column chart on the board similar to the model below. Write a target adjective in column 1 and a collocate noun in column 3.

3. Have students fill in column 2. For each word in column 1, they write an adjective that is opposite in meaning. The opposite must form a correct collocation with the word in column 3.

ADJECTIVES	OPPOSITES	COLLOCATES
simple	*fancy*	meal
simple		task
simple		solution
general		idea
general		knowledge

Sentence-level follow-up:
For each of the word pairs in their charts, have students write a sentence that contrasts the opposite words and expresses an opinion. For example:

> A simple meal like soup and bread might not be fancy, but it can be very satisfying.

2 Computer Collocate Comprehension[11]

Goal: Learners identify words that collocate with computer, discuss their meanings, and list additional collocations that are useful when discussing computers.

Procedure:

1. Distribute copies of the letters below, or create similar letters of your own. Have the class read the letters together.

2. Students work in pairs to identify and list the words that collocate with *computer.*

3. In a class discussion, students (1) identify the meanings of the collocations they identified, and (2) list other words that collocate with *computer.*

4. Then students discuss other computer-related collocations that are used in this passage.

Ask the Computer Geek: Online Advice

Dear Geek,

I was typing my final paper when my computer suddenly froze. I considered shutting it down, but I knew that I hadn't backed up my work. I tried clicking the mouse several times and strange warning messages appeared on the computer screen. The keyboard stopped working. (I also forgot to save the 20 pages I had typed.) I am afraid that if I log off the computer, I won't be able to reboot it. Help! My paper is due tomorrow morning!

Graduating Senior

Dear GS,

The good news is that, if you switch off your computer, you will probably be able to log back on. Please try to turn it off and on again. It's also good news that no one was ever killed by a computer crash. The bad news is that your paper is <u>gone</u>. You didn't mention if your computer is a desktop or a laptop. If it is a laptop computer, try bringing it to my campus office. If this advice doesn't help, please email me again through the Geek website.

Good luck with your final paper.

The Geek

Sentence-level follow-up:
Write a letter back to the Computer Geek, telling him about what has happened since you last wrote, and ask him more questions if necessary. Use 5–10 collocations from the class discussion.

3 Clues for Collocation Collection

Goal: Learners collaborate with each other to generate lists of collocations in different registers, using different parts of speech.

Procedure:

1. Have students work in pairs. Each pair has a sheet of paper.

2. Using the sample clues below (or clues of your own), give students one clue at a time. Ask them to brainstorm words in re-
sponse to your clues, listing as many responses as possible.

Sample Clues

a. words to describe a business meeting (adjectives)

b. words to describe how one might sing (adverbs)

c. words used to describe the possible actions of a professor (verbs)

d. words to describe what can be done with data (verbs)

Sentence-level follow-up:
Students choose one of the following tasks and write an email message, using as many appropriate collocations as possible:

■ Write to your supervisor at work to report on a recent business
meeting.

■ Write to a friend and describe your professor's actions in a recent
class.

4 Metaphorical Ups and Downs

Goal: Learners identify collocations based on the metaphorical patterns
of *up* and *down*.

Procedure:

1. Explain that in English, things that are positive or good often
collocate with words that express the idea of UP (e.g., *Things are
looking up*.). Things that are negative or bad often collocate with
words that express the idea of DOWN (e.g., *Things are at an all-time
low*.).

2. Have the students brainstorm examples. It might help to prompt them with categories, such as status, morality, emotions, etc. Lead a class discussion about the examples.

3. Students look for further examples in both printed material (e.g., newspapers, magazines, online sources) and conversation (e.g., personal interactions, movies, TV dialogue). They share their findings with the class.

5 Why can't you say…?: Connotation versus Animacy

Goal: Learners identify and correct collocation errors due to issues of connotation or animacy.

Procedure:

1. Review the concepts of animacy and connotation with the class. (See pages 41–42 of this chapter.)

2. Students work in pairs to identify the collocation errors in the sentences below, and explain the reason for the error: connotation or animacy.

3. Students then correct the errors without changing the intended meaning of the sentences.

Sentences:

a. Her remarks commanded criticism from the audience.

b. The mechanic told me that my car is incurable.

c. The teacher provoked him to do his best.

d. Her speech inspired us to cry.

e. The tailor operated on the torn sleeve.

6 Functions of Phrases

Goal: Learners identify lexical phrases and the functions they serve.

Procedure:

1. Review with the class some of the functions that lexical phrases perform: express a greeting or a closing; express disagreement;

introduce an example or an exception; explain or give more information; summarize, qualify, or limit the scope of a topic. (See also page 43 of this chapter.)

2. Write a list of lexical phrases on the board. You can use the model below or create your own.

3. Have students read the list and identify the functions of the lexical phrases.

4. Then, students work in pairs to identify other lexical phrases for each function.

LEXICAL PHRASE	FUNCTION
by and large	summarize
That is,	
Hold your horses!	
For the most part	
How ya doing?	
In essence	
While it may be true that	
By and large	
See you later	
On the other hand	

7 Idioms and Lexical Phrases

Goal: Learners identify the errors and the intended meanings in several idioms and lexical phrases. They will also increase their awareness of the universal nature of collocation and fixed expressions.

Procedure:

1. When possible, group students according to common primary languages.

2. Review the meanings of the idioms in the sentences below, through either discussion or guided dictionary practice. Identify the errors in each sentence and clarify how the fixed expressions should read.

3. In their groups, students work to further clarify the meanings of the idioms and to identify similar idioms in their own language. Then, they share their findings with the class.

Sentences

a. Life is not as pink as you might think.

b. The kids were cracking pranks.

c. It's raining dogs and cats.

d. Spare rods, spoil children.

e. Blood is stronger than water.

f. That comes without speaking.

g. When in Rome, do what they do.

Working with Grammatical Features

Grammar is a necessary.
We need it for dominating English.
(Grammar is a necessity. We need it to master English.)

BACKGROUND

It is often hard to tell where word knowledge stops and grammar knowledge begins[1]: grammar provides important information about meaning, and meaning determines how a word is used.[2]

Even as very young children, we use grammar to help us figure out the meaning of a new word. For example, in an experiment using the nonsense word "dax" to mean "doll," two-year-old native English speakers were presented with two sentences: "This is a dax." and "This is dax." The children recognized that in the first sentence, "dax" referred to one of many dolls, while in the second sentence, "dax" referred to the name of one particular doll.[3] That is, they knew that "a" was a signal to show that there was a category called "daxes." Other studies demonstrate how very young children can use a word's part of speech as a clue to its meaning. There is also research showing that children can make inferences about meaning based on whether a verb is transitive or intransitive.[4] Such studies provide strong evidence that children use sentence information to get at meaning before they can use complete sentences, much less understand grammatical explanations.

This ability of children underlines the considerable challenge for English language learners. Native speakers have been observing meaningful patterns of language since birth. They can unconsciously recognize the clues that grammar provides for learning new words, but English language learners may not recognize these clues.

There is a second difficulty for English language learners: their word choices are influenced by the grammatical patterns of their first languages. Therefore, they can be misled by grammatical patterns that they have come to expect. For example, in French, imperative verbs such as *expliquez* (explain) and *racontez* (tell / relate) can be followed by an indirect object without a preposition (*expliquez-moi* and *racontez-moi*), leading the French learner of English to expect

> *Please explain me what is wrong.
> *Please relate me what is wrong.

Similarly, in Russian, there are no equivalents for the English auxiliaries *do*, *have*, *will*, and *be*, leading to learner errors like these:

> * I no like it.
> * When you went there?
> * Do you like football? Yes, I like.[5]

This chapter focuses on the grammatical points that are especially helpful for the teaching and learning of new words. It will help you and your students start to notice more about the ways that words function in English. Remind your students that two-year-olds all over the world are noticing grammatical features in their home languages and are using them to understand new words. Explain that, as older learners, we can train ourselves to do the same.

A CLOSER LOOK AT THE GRAMMATICAL NATURE OF WORDS

1 What Grammar Tells Us about a Word

As we have seen, children learn how to draw meaning from grammar long before they know formal grammar rules. Much of what they know is learned through natural exposure to meaningful language. As teachers, we can emulate this natural process for older learners by providing lots of exposure to meaningful and interactive language experiences on topics that the learners care about. In addition, older learners will benefit if you frequently share your insights about the grammatical behavior of new words.

When we learn a new word, a good starting place is to notice its part of speech (also called its word class).[6] To learn a word's part of speech is to learn something about its role in a given context; this information helps us understand the meaning of both the word and the context. Because parts of speech function differently in different languages, students' assumptions about them will vary greatly. For example, in Spanish, adjectives can be used nearly interchangeably with nouns.[7] In Japanese, there are two classes of adjectives, which operate very differently from each other. Some languages do not distinguish between adjectives and adverbs, and others have no adverbs at all. In addition, many languages have word classes that English does not, such as "measure words" in Chinese and Japanese. Make sure your students can recognize the major parts of speech—nouns, verbs, adjectives, and adverbs—and have an understanding of how they function. As you introduce new vocabulary to your students, be sure to introduce the words' parts of speech as well, along with a lot of sample sentences. Provide ample opportunity for relevant practice, and encourage learners to think of the parts of speech as an important source of meaningful information about words. Demonstrate this to your students with the following sentence. Ask them to identify the parts of speech in each clause:

> Time flies like an arrow; fruit flies like a banana.

2 Noun Grammar Issues

Irregular or unexpected forms

Though research suggests that nouns are the easiest part of speech to learn,[8] they pose particular problems for the student. First, plural forms of nouns can be irregular. For example, nouns that end in *-is* have *-es* in the plural (e.g., *crisis / crises, emphasis / emphases*), and nouns ending in *-um* or *-on* take *-a* in the plural (e.g., *medium / media, criterion / criteria*). In addition, some nouns are always plural (e.g., *clothes, scissors, tropics, jeans, odds*).

A second type of irregularity relates to derivatives. Derivatives are formed when word endings change a part of speech (e.g., *system, systematize, systematic*, etc.). Although there are some endings that are used to mark a word as a noun, such as *-tion*, there are some exceptions. Not knowing the exceptions could lead to errors such as these:

> *No one can bear your demandation. It's too much!
> *We disagreed so strongly that we couldn't come to a compromisation.

See Chapter 5 for further discussion of derivatives.

Count / uncountable forms

Another aspect of noun use that is especially challenging for learners is the notion of countability. When you introduce new nouns in class, be sure to identify them as count nouns (C) or uncountable nouns (U). This feature is critical to a noun's use in that it determines which articles or determiners are appropriate. It also determines verb choice. For example, a singular count noun requires a singular verb.

Make sure your students are familiar with the following rules and constraints.

SINGULAR COUNT NOUNS	PLURAL COUNT NOUNS	UNCOUNTABLE NOUNS
A singular count noun can end in any letter.	A plural count noun usually ends in -*s* or -*es*.	An uncountable noun does not usually end with an -*s* or -*es*.
It can be preceded by *a*, *an*, *one*, or *the*. a table one table	It is preceded by *the* or no article. the tables tables	It cannot be preceded by *a* or *an*. Use *the* or no article. water the water
In the present tense, a singular count noun takes a singular present verb form. *A table usually has four legs.* *One table is enough.*	In the present tense, a plural count noun takes a plural present verb form. *The tables are in the hall.* *Two tables have matching chairs.*	In the present tense, an uncountable noun takes a singular present verb form. *The water is polluted.* *A lot of water flows through this valley.*
	Possible determiners: a few tables a lot of tables a number of tables few tables many tables several tables some tables	Possible determiners: a lot of water a little water little water much water some water

Native speakers of English and some textbooks explain this distinction by saying, "if you can count it, it's a countable noun." Therefore, *chairs* are countable, but *water* is not. Though this guideline is helpful, there are exceptions. For example, consider the confusion between a bag (C) and baggage (U). There can be similar confusion with *fruit, jewelry,* and *clothing,* which are considered uncountable nouns even though we can easily count them as individual items. When you teach patterns of uncountable nouns, focus on patterns of form rather than meaning. Here are four basic structural patterns for uncountable nouns[9]:

■ Nouns that end in *-work*: *homework, course work, work,* but not *framework* or *network*

■ Nouns that end in *-age*: *courage, voltage, postage, luggage, barrage,* but not *garage.*

■ Nouns that end in *-ice*: *advice, malice,* and *ice,* but not *cornice* or *chalice.*

■ Nouns that have the same form as verbs: *air, access, fish, ice, iron, mail, oil, rain, research, slang, snow, smoke, traffic, water, and weather,* but not *approach.*

Your students need to understand that the patterns provide useful guidelines, but they will not always be reliable indications of count-ability. Be sure to point out the exceptions. For example, *research* and *approach* look like they may operate the same way (their noun forms and verb forms are the same), but they don't:

> *There are many approaches to motivation, all based on different researches.

Especially problematic for learners are nouns that have both count and uncountable forms (e.g., *business / businesses, truth / truths*). Sometimes called **crossover nouns,** these words usually have different meanings depending on whether they are countable or uncountable. Learners often confuse the forms and produce sentences such as these:

> *Any kind of <u>dopes</u> at the school are prohibited.
> *The Taj Mahal is made of white <u>marbles</u>.

The distinction between the count and uncountable forms of crossover nouns can be explained by focusing on distinct patterns of meaning differences: Uncountable forms usually refer to a general category, concept, or unit. Count forms usually refer to specific examples, types, servings, units, or individual items.

UNCOUNTABLE FORM	COUNT FORM
business	a business
cheese	a cheese
wine	a wine
time	a time
paper	a paper
coffee	a coffee
aspirin	an aspirin
chocolate	a chocolate
hair	a hair
glass	a glass

3 Verb Grammar Issues

Verbs pose some of the same difficulties for learners as nouns, but they also have their own set of challenges.

Irregular or unexpected forms

Verbs can have irregular past tense forms. Not knowing these forms can lead to learner errors like these:

> *I goed to the airport to pick up my dad.
> *These shoes costed $85.00.

Also, as is true for all parts of speech, we can't always rely on the derivative endings that usually help us recognize a word as a verb. For example, -*ate* and -*ize* are often used as verb-forming suffixes (e.g., *congratulate, agitate, humiliate, memorize, familiarize, plagiarize*). When learners apply this pattern where it doesn't belong, however, they can produce sentences such as these:

> *I am considerate going to Mexico for my vacation.
> *It's interesting when you observate cultural differences.
> *The teacher was the first to notarize the problem.

See Chapter 5 for further discussion of derivatives.

Misleading meanings

Some words can be misleading because they appear to follow the patterns of verbs, but they don't function as verbs. For example, the learner who knows the verb *mention* might infer that the following sentence is acceptable:

> *I went to only one coed elementary school, as I aforementioned.

Similarly, there are some nouns that can be misleading because they suggest action, but they are not verbs. This leads to learner errors like these:

> *I can ride you.
> *I cannot revenge.
> *He suicided in 1938.

These errors are indications of partial knowledge and are indeed "intelligent errors"—the learner clearly knows that the role of verbs is to express action. What went wrong was the use of the parts of speech. Learners need to be able to identify parts of speech accurately. They also need to know that sometimes we need collocations to express what we mean (*give a ride, take revenge, commit suicide*).

Transitive / intransitive verbs

A transitive verb is a verb that requires an object. The object cannot be part of a prepositional phrase. If the learner doesn't know this, they might say,

> *We interviewed to 29 people.

An intransitive verb does not require an object. Instead of saying *He worried* or *He worried about buying a house*, the learner might guess,

> *He worried the house.

Some verbs pose particular problems in that they can be both transitive and intransitive.

> I accepted the invitation.
> Thanks for the invitation. I accept.

Learners also have to know that only transitive verbs can be used in passive sentences:

> The people were interviewed.
> The invitation was accepted.
> *Buying a house was worried about.

Another important rule is that some transitive verbs cannot be made into passives, including verbs of measure, reciprocal verbs, and verbs of fitting.[10] For example:

> *100 pounds is weighed by me.
> *Steve is resembled by his son.
> *I am fit by a size 9.

Complements

The part of a sentence that follows a verb, thus completing the verb, is called a complement. Different verbs require different types of complements. As learners learn a new verb, they need to notice how it is completed. Sample sentences in the dictionary are often a good source of this information. There are several types of common complements that students should learn.

Infinitives and gerunds: Some verbs are followed by infinitives (e.g., *to learn*); others by gerunds (e.g., *learning*); and others can be followed by either.[11]

VERB + COMPLEMENT	EXAMPLES[12]
verb + infinitive	choose, dare, expect, fail, hope, manage, proceed, promise, refuse, tend, want, vow
verb + gerund	admit, appreciate, avoid, deny, dislike, enjoy, finish, quit, recall, resume, risk
verb + either infinitive or gerund	begin, continue, forget, hate, intend, like, love, prefer, remember, start, try

Errors often result when learners don't understand these restrictions on verbs or when they misuse the forms:

> *I do not want bother her.
> *We expect her coming soon.
> *Whenever my brother finishes to study, he plays games.

***That*-clauses**: Some verbs require a *that*-clause for their completion:

> We <u>ask</u> that you help us.
> We <u>think </u>that you should help us.
> We <u>hope</u> that you will help us.

That-clauses appear most often with verbs of cognition (e.g., *think, know, believe*), perception (e.g., *see, hear*), and speech (e.g., *say, report*). They appear to be somewhat frequent in conversation and in fiction writing, and less frequent in academic writing.[13]

When you point out a pattern that is complicated, be sure to avoid long grammatical explanations. Just note a detail or two, and then present some sample sentences. For example, "*Ask* can be followed by either an object or by a *that*-clause: *He asked a question* or *She asked that we come at 5:00.*" Consider using online concordancers when you cover verb complements. They will provide an assortment of authentic sentences and will help make patterns of use clear. Select a verb that often causes learners confusion when they have to choose an appropriate complement. For example, some students have difficulty with *suggest*.

> *I suggest her to join a club.

The concordance lines will show examples of the target verb from authentic sources:

12	ield. There is also no evidence to	suggest	that the crosses were destroyed by
13	requires a complete side room to	suggest	the strangulation of the urban by
14	mford, but there is no evidence to	suggest	they were ever used by man. In 184
15	were looking for a shrub, I would	suggest	Chimonanthus praecox , or winter
16	s are listed in London. This would	suggest	that sterling eurobonds not listed
18	ia FIRST PLANTINGS Q Can you	suggest	one or two attractive winter flower
19	HOUSE PLANTS Q Please could you	suggest	some house plants for my bedroom w

You can find concordance lines such as these by searching on the Internet for "online concordancers." See Chapter 3 for guidelines on using concordancers.

Phrasal verbs

Phrasal verbs are very common in English, but few non-Germanic languages use them. They usually consist of a one-syllable verb (e.g., *go, count, take*), followed by an adverb, preposition, or both (e.g., *away, apart, together, in, over, out, on, off*). Phrasal verbs cause confusion because their meanings are often not clear from their parts; for example, in the phrasal verb *give up*, nobody "gives" and nothing goes "up." Learner errors give us insight into the difficulties:

> *Don't pick up the flowers in the park.
>
> *She's always prepared. You can count in her.
>
> *The doctor told me to cut sugar down.
>
> *Please don't throw that letter. I want to keep it.

4 Adjective and Adverb Grammar Issues

Adjectives and adverbs function very differently (or don't appear at all) in many other languages. They pose a variety of problems for the word learner.

Unexpected forms

Learners who depend on word parts to make sense of adjective meanings will find many exceptions. A few endings seem predictable for adjectives (e.g., *-y*, as in *worthy, pricey, filthy*), but they don't always work.

> *I am so nervous it makes me have a difficulty time.
>
> *This was a very influency class.

The *-ly* ending is frequently used for adverbs, but not all adverbs end in *-ly* (e.g., *fast, slow, tomorrow*) and not all words ending in *-ly* are adverbs (e.g., *friendly, leisurely, ugly, family*). Adverbs of manner (e.g., *happily, slowly*) usually end in *-ly*, whereas adverbs of direction (e.g., *there*), location (e.g., *crosswise*), time (e.g., *soon*), and frequency (e.g., *often*) are less predictable. Many student errors result from an assumption that all adverbs use the *-ly* ending:

> *Don't walk so fastly. I can't keep up.
>
> *The birds are flying highly in the sky.

Misleading meanings

There are many modifiers (adjectives and adverbs) that can be confused with one another because their forms are similar; however, their meanings and functions differ. For example, *loudly* and *aloud* are both adverbs, but they have different meanings. A confusion of these words is reflected in the following sentence. The student intended to refer to oral reading when she wrote,

> *They read the paragraph loudly. (meaning *aloud*)

Similarly, the adverbs *late* and *lately* have different meanings, as do *hard* and *hardly* and *high* and *highly*. Though the following sentences looks structurally correct, they are not meaningful:

> *We wake up lately.
> *My mother works hardly.
> *She studied hardly for the test.
> *They camped highly up on the hill.

Intensifiers… and the company they keep

As students learn new adjectives, it is helpful for them to know how they can adjust the degrees of the description (e.g., *slightly embarrassed, somewhat embarrassed, very embarrassed, extremely embarrassed*). Encourage learners to add variety to their language use by not limiting themselves to the commonly used intensifiers *very* and *too*. Other adverbs that can vary an adjective's intensity (both to make words stronger and to make them weaker) include *absolutely, completely, clearly, extremely, markedly, totally, slightly, a little*, and *somewhat*. The difficulty of using these adverbs is reflected in the following student errors:

> *He is completely thirsty.
> *She is absolutely tired / intelligent / rich.
> *We got clearly / markedly lost.
> *She's a little beautiful.
> *They're slightly rich.

Though *exactly* is not usually considered an intensifier, it can be misperceived as one, leading to errors such as this:

> *Chinese and Americans are exactly different.

It is wise to advise learners that certain adverbs of degree and adjectives don't collocate, making some phrases awkward. In some cases, dictionaries can help. You can also help by introducing modifiers that collocate with new target words. See Chapter 3 for further discussion of collocations.

5 Part-of-Speech Conversions

An additional challenge for the English language learner is that new words are often formed by converting one part of speech into another.[14] Sometimes a verb has changed into a noun (e.g., *This book is a good read*.). Interestingly, it is more common for nouns to become verbs.[15] Some examples of verbs that started out as nouns:

to butter	to water	to dust	to kennel
to access	to email	to fax	to carpool
to party	to medal	to breakfast	to lunch

Explain to learners that this feature is a natural part of language change, and encourage them to be on the lookout for it. When learners form sentences such as the following, they are making intelligent, albeit incorrect, guesses based on their observations:

*It is rude to bubble the gum in someone's face.
*Did you needle the pants yet? (mend)
*He dinners with our family.
*He is keying the door. (locking)

6 Words with the Same Meaning but Different Behavior

It is important to remember that there is a grammatical challenge when you look up a word in the dictionary and find a choice of synonyms. At first glance, this list of synonyms may seem helpful, but it is unlikely that you could use all the synonyms in a sentence in the same way. For example, if you look up the verb *change*, your dictionary might offer the choices *alter, turn*, or *convert*. These are indeed synonyms, but they differ in the ways that they behave in a sentence. For example, only one of the verbs can complete the sentence *When I heat the liquid, it _____ thick*. The verbs all require different types of complements; only *turn* can occur with an adjective complement.[16]

Learners encounter this kind of challenge all the time. For example, they might find that *little* and *brief* are synonyms, but the following sentences show that they are not at all the same grammatically:

* I know very brief about my mother's family.
* I have brief respect for people who don't recycle.

Similarly, *speak, talk,* and *say* have very similar meanings, which can lead to the following confusions of verbs:

*It makes me feel uncomfortable if they understand what I am talking.
*I didn't have much to speak.

Take a few minutes to make your own observations about this feature of language. Look up a few synonyms in a thesaurus, and experiment by using the words you find in sentences. For example, look up the verb *consider.* Your thesaurus may include *think, believe, deem, judge,* and *regard as.* You will first notice that there are subtle differences in meaning and formality. Then think about the following sentences, this time focusing on the many grammatical differences:

a. She never considered nursing as a career option.

   Consider is a transitive verb. *Nursing* is the object, which is completed by a prepositional phrase.

b. *She never thought nursing as a career option.

   Thought is intransitive. It requires a prepositional phrase or a sentence-complement: *She never thought about nursing as a career option* or *She never thought (that) she would be a nurse.*

c. *She didn't believe nursing as a career option.

   Believe can be either transitive or intransitive, but when used transitively as in the example, it cannot be followed with a prepositional phrase beginning with *at.* One might say *She never believed in nursing as a career option,* but this changes the meaning of sentence a.

Your students need to understand that no two words are exactly the same. In fact, there is a good reason for that: in order for two words to survive in a language, they must have something to distinguish them from one another. One way synonyms vary is by having very distinct grammatical tendencies that determine how they function in sentences.

KEY CONSIDERATIONS FOR THE CLASSROOM

1 Be Aware of the Grammatical Learning Burden

As noted earlier, the difficulty that a word poses is its *learning burden*[17]; some words are just more difficult to learn than others. The grammatical learning burden is heavier for words with particular features. For example, words with irregular plural and past tense forms are harder to learn than words with regular forms. Adjectives and adverbs are harder to learn than nouns and verbs. In addition, the learning burden is heavier for patterns or features that don't appear in a learner's first language.

See Chapter 1 for further discussion of the learning burden.

2 Introduce New Words with Grammatical Clues

You don't need to explicitly state the part of speech of every new word. Instead, help your students learn how to identify the parts of speech themselves by using clues that you provide. For example,

- when you introduce a countable noun, use *a / an* (*an idea*)

- when you introduce a verb, use *to* (*to demonstrate*)

- when you introduce an adjective, use *to be* (*to be jealous*)

- when a word is commonly followed by a certain preposition, include that preposition in your introduction of the word (*to discriminate against, to collaborate with, to rely on*).[18]

Simple, implicit clues such as these can help learners notice context and assist them in becoming independent word learners.

3 Teach Learners How to Use Grammatical Information in Dictionaries

Students don't often take full advantage of the grammatical information in their dictionaries. Most good dictionaries of English indicate parts of speech, regular and irregular forms of nouns and verbs, and transitive and intransitive verbs. Dictionaries specially designed for English language learners (learner dictionaries) usually also include information about noun countability, phrasal verbs, and preposition use. As you clarify these features, show your students how such grammatical information can be of great help as they practice using new words.

See Chapter 7 for further discussion of dictionary selection and use.

ACTIVITIES

1 A Picture Tells a Story

Goal: Learners identify the parts of speech of target words and prepare to use them in a description.

Procedure:

1. Write a four-column chart on the board and label the columns with the parts of speech as shown in the model below.

2. Select a picture (from a book, a magazine, or the Internet) that could inspire an interesting story.

3. Brainstorm with the class 10–15 words that would be useful in describing or asking questions about the picture. Then, as a class, select 3–5 words from that list to use in this activity. Write each word in the appropriate column of the chart, according to its part of speech.

4. When all the words are on the board, have students brainstorm words related to each target word (i.e., word family members). Write each word in the appropriate column. Mark an X in each column that has no word form that fits.

NOUNS	VERBS	ADJECTIVES	ADVERBS
endurance	endure	enduring	X
belief	believe	believing believable	believably
seriousness	X	serious	seriously

Note: Sample words in chart are based on the painting, *American Gothic*, by Grant Wood.

Sentence-level follow-up:

Students work in pairs to create a story about the picture, including any of the forms of the words in the chart.

OR

Use this as a pre-reading prediction activity. Select a picture that is related to a text that the class is about to read. First, have pairs brainstorm words that they would use to express predictions about the text. Next, they prepare a chart of target and related words. Finally, students write either questions about the text or predictions about what they expect to find, and share their sentences with the class. For more practice, give each pair of students a new picture, and have them repeat the process.

2 Noun Countdown

Goal: Learners list the nouns that are used in a news report, and then identify whether they are countable or uncountable.

Procedure:

1. Select an interesting, current video or audio news segment (about one minute long).

2. Review the concepts of count and uncountable nouns, reminding students about the articles and verb forms that are used with each. (See pages 58–60 of this chapter.)

3. Students listen to the taped segment and list as many nouns as possible. If you are using a video, turn off the picture to help students focus. Encourage students to listen for clues, including pronunciation, singular or plural verb forms, and article usage. Demonstrate by playing a short segment and explaining how you identified the nouns as countable or not.

4. Students work in pairs to compare lists and clarify meanings.

5. Students listen to the segment again, this time writing the articles and endings. Working in pairs, they label each noun they have listed as count or uncountable [e.g., the weather (U), a storm front (C), the clouds (C)]. Students can also add more nouns to their lists at this time.

6. Students discuss their lists with the class, focusing on the clues of countability and clarifying meaning as needed.

Sentence-level follow-up:

In pairs, students write a summary of the news segment, using the nouns in their lists. When you proofread the summaries, pay particular attention to the countability of the nouns, including article use, the plural ending of the nouns, and the verb choices.

3 Countability Confusion

Goal: Learners identify the difference in meanings between nouns that have both count and uncountable forms.

Procedure:

1. Review, with the class, the grammatical behavior of count and uncountable nouns. (See pages 58–60 of this chapter.)

2. Refer to the list of nouns on page 60, and write it on the board or on an overhead transparency. Working in pairs, students write sentences using both count and uncountable forms of each noun. For example, *business* (U) could refer to a career in business. A *business* (C) could refer to a software company. Students can use their dictionaries as needed.

3. Students discuss their sentences with the class, focusing on the patterns of meaning difference.

Sentence-level follow-up:

Students select five of the count-uncountable word pairs on the board, and for each word they write a question that contrasts the meanings.

> **Example**
>
> After you finish your degree in <u>business</u>, do you want to start <u>a business</u> of your own?

4 How regular is verb regularity?

Goal: Learners examine the forms of selected verbs and identify patterns of regularity.

Procedure:

1. Write a three-column chart on the board similar to the model below. Label the columns as shown.

2. Give students a list of about ten recently studied verbs. Be sure that the list contains a mix of regular and irregular verbs. List some verbs in the present, some in the past, and some in the past participle form.

3. Students work in pairs to write the words in the appropriate columns of the chart; then they fill in the remaining columns with the correct verb forms, using their dictionaries as needed.

PRESENT	PAST	PAST PARTICIPLE
	examined	
		known
say		
		chosen
entitle (to)		

Sentence-level follow-up:

1. Select a topic that fits the words selected. Consider topics from class discussions, recent readings, high-interest current events, or campus news.

2. Write five questions about the topic, using the appropriate verb forms in the chart. (Include yes/no and information questions.)

3. Working in pairs, students ask and answer the questions in complete sentences. Each pair then writes a sample question and answer on the board for class discussion.

5 Are you complementing my verb?

Goal: Learners watch a video and list the verbs that describe the actions they see. Then, they identify whether the verbs are transitive or not, and how they are used (including transitivity of verbs and complements).

Procedure:

1. Select an interesting video segment that has several characters and a lot of action (about one minute long).

2. Review the concepts of verb forms and complements with the class. (See pages 60–63 of this chapter.)

3. Students watch the taped segment with the sound turned off and list verbs that describe the actions they see (*laughing, asking, throwing,* etc.).

4. Working in pairs, students compare lists and clarify meanings.

5. They watch the segment again, adding more verbs to their lists.

6. In pairs, students review their lists and extend them into short phrases, such as *laughed at his sister, threw the ball, broke the window,* and *asked about the accident.* Dictionaries can be used as needed.

7. Play the segment again, this time with the sound turned on. Students add new words and details to the lists.

8. Students discuss their lists with the class, focusing on verb complements.

Sentence-level follow-up:

1. Working in pairs, students write a summary of the video segment in the present tense, using the verb phrases in their lists.

2. Each pair exchanges their summary with another pair, who then writes their classmates' summary in the past tense.

6 Why can't you say…?

Goal: Learners identify and correct verb complement errors.

Procedure:

1. Review the concept of complements with the class. (See pages 62–64 of this chapter.)

2. Write the following sentences on the board (without the asterisks), or create similar sentences of your own:
   a. *I <u>want</u> that my mother will come.
   b. *They <u>forced</u> him that he confess.
   c. *I <u>understood</u> me being the winner.
   d. *The interviewer <u>insisted</u> me to stay for lunch.
   e. *They <u>disagreed</u> going to the movie.
   f. *He enjoys to play the piano.

3. Students work in pairs to identify the complement errors, and explain the reasons for the errors. Dictionaries can be used, as needed, to identify appropriate complements: infinitive, gerund, *that*-clause, or prepositional phrase.

4. Then, students correct the errors in the sentences without changing meaning.

7 More about That Verb

Goal: Learners review familiar verbs and determine the forms needed to complete them in a sentence.

Procedure:

1. Provide students with a list of about ten recently studied verbs. Be sure the list contains a mix of transitive verbs, intransitive verbs, and verbs that are both.

2. Write the words on the board in simple sentences, as shown in this sample:

> He abolished.
> He reacted.
> He advocated.
> He concentrated.

3. Students work in pairs to determine whether each sentence is complete as is, or whether it needs a complement. Dictionaries can be used as needed.

4. In a class discussion, have students consider various ways to extend each sentence.

8 What do people really say?

Goal: Learners examine samples of authentic language through online concordancers, and identify patterns of use among verb complements and modifiers.

Procedure:

1. This activity works best in a computer lab with two or three students assigned to each computer. Begin by searching the Internet to find an "online concordancer," or use the following:

   Cobb, Tom. *The Compleat Lexical Tutor*. 2006.
   http://www.lextutor.ca (accessed October 2007).

2. Provide students with a list of about five recently studied words that seem to be especially challenging for them. (See pages 8–9 from Chapter 1 and page 68 of this chapter to review the concept of a word's learning burden.)

3. Demonstrate how to view about 30 sentences for each word, and how to use the concordance lines.

4. Working in pairs or small groups, students examine the concordance lines to answer the following questions:

   Nouns

   a. Is this a count noun or an uncountable noun? How do you know?

   b. Do you see any patterns in the ways that articles are used with this noun?

   c. Are there any adjectives used more than once with this noun?

   d. Do you see any other patterns that occur frequently with this noun?

   Verbs

   a. Do you see any patterns for the completion of this verb?

   b Are there any adverbs that are used more than once with this verb?

   c. Do you see any other patterns that frequently occur with this verb?

   For an example, refer to the sample concordance lines for *suggest* (on page 63 of this chapter). The patterns include: *suggest + that*-clause, *suggest + noun, evidence + to suggest, would + suggest, can / could + you suggest.*

Sentence-level follow-up:

Write the target words on the board. Arrange groups of about 6–8 students in individual circles. Students take turns asking questions of their group. Every question and answer must use a target word. Encourage students to ask interesting questions that are relevant to their lives. Continue until everyone has asked and answered at least one question and every target word has been used.

Examples

What do you suggest that I eat for dinner?

If I were to travel to Korea, where do you suggest I visit?

Working with Word Parts CHAPTER 5

Detergents bewilder assistants.

Deter gents! Be wilder! Assist ants!

BACKGROUND

Word parts can't be trusted. Or can they? The sentences above show that many English words are made up of smaller words, but the parts don't necessarily inform us about the whole. To the learner who is relying on word parts for meaning, many combinations can appear to be something they are not: *beanstalk: beans talk; manslaughter: man's laughter; nowhere: now here; bargain: bar gain; surgeon: surge on; roughage: rough age.* It isn't always easy to know when you can trust the parts of words and when they will mislead you.

Sometimes patterns of word parts seem clear: *meaningful = meaning + ful,* indicating "full of meaning." The opposite of *meaningful* is *meaningless.* The same pattern occurs with *hopeful / hopeless* and *merciful / merciless.* But our trust is tested as we gather language experience: What's the opposite of a *beautiful sunset?* Or a *seamless garment?* Or a *horseless carriage?* And aren't *shameless* and *shameful* actually similar in meaning?

Some words are confusing because their relationship is not what it seems. For example, although *button* and *unbutton* are opposites, *ravel* and *unravel* are the same, as are *loosen* and *unloosen.* Still other word pairs with negative prefixes are neither opposites nor the same: *pertinent / impertinent, canny / uncanny,* and *famous / infamous.*[1] Many words clearly seem to be related but they aren't: *adult / adultery; infant / infantry.* Proficient speakers take these inconsistencies in stride, but they pose considerable challenges to the English language learner, who is trying to figure out which word parts are reliable and which are not.

Research demonstrates that problems often occur when English language learners recognize word parts and then use their prior knowledge to help them figure out the meaning. For example, in studies of second language readers, *infallible* was read as *in* + *fall* + *ible*, and interpreted as "something that cannot fall." *Shortcomings* was read as *short* + *comings* and interpreted as "short visits." *Outline* was understood as "out of line," *falsities* as "false cities," and *discourse* as "without direction."[2] These logical guesses remind us of the great difficulty that learners face when decoding new words.

While word parts pose many such challenges, we cannot ignore them as a resource for learning. Studies show that native speaking children learn as many as 3,000 new words a year through elementary school. This sizeable accomplishment is at least partially explained by the children's abilities to use their knowledge of word parts to relate familiar words to new ones.[3] Word parts are also the means by which we identify words that belong to the same family (e.g., *comfort, discomfort, comforter, (un)comfortable*) or words that function as the same part of speech (e.g., *capable, palpable,* and *responsible* are adjectives). As a result, word parts help us guess the meanings of new words from context. Studying word parts helps us classify them for future use. In addition, word parts help us store words in memory. Research shows that when we are trying to recall a word, we sometimes access it according to its prefix, suffix, or root.[4] All this evidence suggests that an understanding of word parts and their relationship to word families will help learners access and retain words.

A good word learner acquires a balanced view of reality: word parts can be both informative and misleading. It's the job of the teacher and the student to learn how to recognize when words follow frequent, regular patterns and when they don't.

A CLOSER LOOK AT THE PARTS OF WORDS

1 Word Parts: What They Are and What They Do

Keep your explanations of how words are formed as simple as possible. Your goals should be (1) to provide enough information to enable students to notice patterns, and (2) to provide enough terminology to enable them to discuss their observations. Students should learn a few basic terms that will enable them to notice and talk about word formation.

- **root:** the part of a word that carries the main meaning and that other forms are based on.
- **affix:** refers to both a **prefix** (at the beginning of a word) and a **suffix** (at the end of a word).

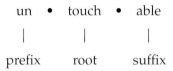

- **compound:** a combination of two or more roots (e.g., *wheelchair*).

There are three basic ways that word parts are combined in English: prefixing, suffixing, and compounding.

Prefixing

Adding a prefix to a word usually changes its meaning. (e.g., *review, unavailable, discomfort*). Occasionally, prefixes change a word's part of speech (e.g., *able / enable; dear / endear*), but that is unusual. Prefixing is difficult for learners because it does not follow consistent patterns. For example, although *mis-*, *dis-*, and *un-* are used to indicate the negative (e.g., *misunderstand, dislike, unable*), they are not interchangeable. When learners try to use these prefixes interchangeably or otherwise inappropriately, problems can occur:

> *We regret that you will be misconvenienced.
> *He unlikes to be late for class.
> *Take one of our horse-driven city tours. We guarantee no miscarriages.

Similarly, the prefix *re-* can be added to a root or to a verb to mean *again, anew,* or *back* (e.g., *remove, restate, resell*), but it can't be added to words indiscriminately:

> * She was moved by the sad movie; when she saw it again, she was removed (moved again).
> * We need to know more about the robbery to stop recrime.

Suffixing

Adding a suffix to a word can serve two functions: it creates **inflections** or **derivations**. An inflection results when a suffix changes a word's grammatical function without changing its part of speech. For example, the addition of -*s* or -*es* to a noun makes it plural (e.g., *ocean / oceans; box / boxes*). The addition of -*ed* can change a verb to past tense (e.g., *create / created*). Inflections are easier than derivations for both proficient speakers of English and learners because they often follow rules and are somewhat consistent. Inflections are also common in both oral and written language, so learners have considerable exposure to them.[5]

A derivation results when an affix (usually a suffix) is added to change a word's part of speech (e.g., *communicate, communication, communicative*). Derivations are very challenging for learners because there are many different suffixes that serve the same function. For example, -*ity*, -*ness*, -*ment*, and -*tion* are just some of the noun-forming suffixes. Also, the formation of derivations is not governed by consistent rules. For example, although -*ness* and -*ity* / -*ty* are both common noun-forming suffixes, they usually cannot be used interchangeably:

*The difficultness of the exercise is great.

*The complexness of the problem was overwhelming.

Sometimes confusion occurs because learners see derivational patterns with some words, and try to apply them to others. For example, the verb form of *quick* is *quicken*, but the verb form of *fast* (*meaning quick*) is not *fasten*. The verb form of *length* is *lengthen*, but the verb form of *long* is not *longen*. Similarly, in order to change the noun *dictation* to a verb, you have to remove the noun suffix -*tion* (e.g., *dictate*). But, the same pattern does not hold when you change the noun *solution*:

*I hope to solute this problem.

Derivations are also more difficult because they are relatively less frequent in oral language than in written language, so learners have less exposure to them. Research suggests that "even very advanced users of English are likely to have gaps in their derivational knowledge."[6]

Compounding

Forming **compound words** tends to be easier for students to master, but compounds do pose certain problems. They are less clear to some learners than you might think, as indicated in these creative errors:

*She used an electric chair after the car accident.

*When I want a tan, I take a sunshower.

The written form of compounds can be confusing because they can be written as two separate words, as a hyphenated word, or as one word (e.g., *outstanding, easy-going, night owl*). In some cases, there is no standardized written form (e.g., *freeze dry, freeze-dry,* or *freezedry*). Many new words have entered the English language through compounding, and the process continues; it is important that learners know that they are likely to see variations.

2 Using Word Parts

The skills learners need

Using word parts effectively, or **word building,** requires specific skills. Learners must recognize several things:that words are made of meaningful parts

■ the meanings of the parts

■ that changes occur when parts are combined

■ how to interpret the combined meaning of the parts.[7]

These steps pose many difficulties. Many student errors result from the misuse of a recognized pattern:

* There are merits to this decision, but there are also demerits.

* They felt dignant.

* Do you have time to complete the questionary? (questionnaire)

An important skill that you should encourage during word-building practice is careful and effective dictionary use. Dictionaries can help learners avoid inaccurate guesses and confirm accurate ones. See Chapter 7 for further discussion of dictionary use.

Making use of patterns

Because word formation is not always governed by predictable rules, the use of affixes is bound to be inconsistent. There are some patterns that occur fairly frequently, and these may be helpful to the learner, but even they must be used with caution. You may choose to let students acquire the patterns naturally, through experience with language, much as native speakers do. Or you may want to point out some of the following tendencies of word building.

There are some suffixes that tend to attach to **standalone words** only. (A standalone word doesn't need a suffix in order to function as an independent word; e.g., *happy, teach, priority, govern*.) The addition of these suffixes (e.g., *-ness, -er, -ize, -ment*) does not usually cause a change in stress or vowel sound. They also do not tend to alter the meaning of the affixed word; its meaning is clearly related to the original word (e.g., *happiness, teacher, prioritize, government*).

There are other suffixes (e.g., *-ity, -ify, -ous, -ive, -y, -al*) that often attach to roots that are not standalone words (e.g., *gratify, qualify, generous*). This kind of suffix often causes a change of stress and/or vowel sound (e.g., *profane / profanity*). It also tends to change the meaning of the affixed word, whose meaning is often not clearly related to the root (e.g., *native / nativity, confide / confident, virtue / virtual*).

Here are a few other tendencies that might be helpful to learners:

- *-ness* usually attaches to adjectives but not to verbs (e.g., *quietness, playfulness;* but not **playness*)

- *-ly* can be added to adjectives but not to nouns

- *re-* is more often attached to transitive verbs (e.g., *remove, retake, refill*) than to intransitive verbs (e.g., **restand, *resmoke, *recome*).

Explaining some of the tendencies of word building may help students recognize reliable patterns. Explanations alone, however, are insufficient. Students need opportunities to experiment with word-building skills. You might try handing out a list of productive prefixes, and have students compile a list of words using them.[8] Then have the class compare the function of the prefixes in the various examples. Students might also use a list of productive prefixes to generate "new" or made-up words; these can be used to demonstrate how word building can be used for literary effects, marketing purposes, or humor.[9] Through activities like these, students will gradually learn how word building works, and they will start to look for patterns on their own.

3 Affixation Causes Other Changes

Adding affixes is not as mechanical as putting together puzzle pieces. The addition of affixes to a word can change its spelling, pronunciation, and meaning.

Spelling changes

Adding a prefix to a word is usually straightforward; the prefix and the stem stay the same (e.g., *mis* + *take* = *mistake*; *dis* + *approve* = *disapprove*). Adding suffixes, however, usually causes changes in spelling (e.g., *mystery* + *ous* = *mysterious*; *value* + *able* = *valuable*). You may choose to avoid rules and have learners make generalizations on their own, as they tend to do. Or you might like to point out a few examples of spelling rules. A few carefully selected spelling rules may help learners recognize that, although English spelling is difficult, it is not completely haphazard. (Note that there will always be exceptions.[10]) For example:

ADDING A SUFFIX TO A WORD ENDING IN "Y"[11]		
When the "y" is preceded by a consonant	change the "y" to "i" before adding the suffix	curly / curlier party / parties thirty / thirtieth beauty / beautiful dry / dried happy / happiest
When the "y" is preceded by a vowel	do not change the "y" to "i"	journey / journeying trolley / trolleys play / player
Exception: When the suffix begins with "i"	do not change the "y" to "i" (before the suffix "-ize" or "-ization," drop the "y")	thirty / thirtyish fry / frying agony / agonize memory / memorization

Pronunciation changes

Recognizing word parts in spoken language can be difficult because they can be disguised by changes in pronunciation. Sometimes, changes in stress occur when affixes are added (e.g., *civil / civility; moral / morality; captive / captivity*). Change can also occur in vowel sounds (e.g., *reduce / reduction; describe / description; south / southern*).

There are a few regularities that you might want to point out:

▪ In some words, the /k/ sound in the adjective becomes /s/ in the noun:

electric   →   electricity

authentic   →   authenticity

domestic   →   domesticity

public   →   publicity

- For some words, there are stress changes when the parts of speech change:

an OBject	→	to obJECT
a DEcrease	→	to deCREASE
PERfect	→	to perFECT
a PERmit	→	to perMIT
a CONflict	→	to conFLICT

Meaning changes

When different affixes are added to the same root, the result may be two words with very different meanings even though the words look like members of the same family (e.g., *consideration / considerable, proceeds* (noun) */ procedure, bonding / bondage*). Learners have particular trouble distinguishing between related derivations that are the same part of speech (e.g., *media / mediation, hospitable / hospitalized, consumed / consummated*).[12] This can lead to unfortunate confusion:

*Please leave your values at the front desk.

*The car was spewing exhaustion.

*Every step of the process was automotive.

Meaning changes such as these can be subtle but important. You can use them to discuss the difficulties of word building as students practice.

4 Caveats Concerning the Teaching of Roots and Affixes

The explicit teaching of roots and affixes is not appropriate for every group of students. Think about your particular situation and weigh the pros and cons.

When you do choose to teach particular roots and affixes, remember that some are more useful than others. A few well-chosen affixes can equip students to deal with the parts of speech and meanings of many words. Remember, native English speaking children learn as many as 3,000 words per year, in part because they use familiar word parts to make sense of new words. Also, research suggests that good readers are more aware of word parts than are poor readers.[13]

One factor that should influence how and whether you directly teach roots and affixes is the language background of your students. The idea of roots and affixes will be more familiar and intuitive to the speakers of some languages than to others. For example, in Vietnamese, Samoan, or Chinese, words have no endings; grammatical relationships are expressed by word order. The concept of using word parts to express grammar differences is new, as are the word parts themselves. It is harder to tease apart words and analyze them accurately when one is learning the process of word building as well as the word parts themselves.

Another factor to consider is the level of your students. Word parts are more useful to students with larger vocabularies. If a learner does not know the word *capable,* then it won't be helpful to know that *incapable* is its opposite. Similarly, learners who know the multiple meanings of words will be more successful in making sense of the changes that come with affixes. For example, the words *discontent* and *contentment* cannot be guessed accurately if you don't know the meaning of the adjective *content* ("happy or satisfied").

In the end, teachers should be prepared to adapt instruction to the needs of each group. Word parts are too important to ignore and too inconsistent to abide by blindly. We can offer our students an important layer of word knowledge by acknowledging both consistent patterns and exceptions. Both are part of the reality of word building.

KEY CONSIDERATIONS FOR THE CLASSROOM

1 Be Selective about the Roots and Affixes You Teach

It isn't realistic, efficient, or even interesting to try to teach all affixes. Learn how to make good choices. Be aware of which word parts are the easiest to learn and the most frequent. For example, when the base form is a word in its own right, word building is easier for learners.[14] Likewise, the easiest and most useful affixes are those which occur in many words (especially commonly used words) and those with predictable meanings, pronunciation, and spelling.

The following 14 suffixes are good choices because they are found in more than 60% of the words with suffixes on the General Service List (the most frequent 2,000 word families in English).[15]

Noun suffixes	Verb suffixes	Adjective suffixes
-ness	*-en*	*-less*
-er / -or	*-ise / -ize*	*-al*
-ty / -ity		*-y*
-ance / -ence		*-ful*
-ion		*-ward*
-ment		*-ern*

Similarly, the following prefixes are found in 66% of the prefixed words in printed school materials.[16]

Noun prefixes	Verb prefixes	Adjective prefixes
un-	*re-*	*in- / im- / il- / -ir*
dis-		*en- / em-*
		non-

2 Remember That Familiar Words Play a Crucial Role

Nation often says that the most important part of any lesson is not the new material that you present, but the old. This is true for several reasons.[17] First, if you don't review old material, it will be forgotten. Students will have, at best, only partial mastery of the old material, so a return to it will deepen their understanding. Especially significant for us, as teachers of vocabulary, is the fact that familiar information gives learners a firm basis for processing new information. That is, familiar words enable learners to make predictions about both meaning and structural patterns, including roots and affixes.

When teachers review old material or elicit information from students, they assist this process. For example, when introducing a new topic in class, elicit from the class a list of previously studied words that might be used to discuss the new topic. As you write them on the board, list them according to their parts of speech. Use this review to discuss patterns of meaning (e.g., "Do you think this topic will be as *controversial* as the last one?") and form (e.g., "What part of speech is *controversial*? What other adjectives have the same suffix?").

Discussions using familiar information can also help learners deal with exceptions to patterns and to the many choices for expressing the same thing (e.g., "What are some of the other suffixes used to form an adjective?"). We can facilitate pattern recognition and help learners make effective generalizations by using familiar examples to illustrate new relationships.

3 Be Aware of Learner Avoidance

If your students are not making many errors with word parts, that doesn't necessarily mean that they are mastering them. In fact, they may be avoiding them. Research suggests that learners tend to avoid using a derived form when a simpler form is available.[18] They also tend to avoid forms that are difficult to pronounce.[19] (Remember that word form changes can include pronunciation changes.)

It is therefore especially important to help our students understand word building and increase their confidence by encouraging them to experiment. The counterpart to that, of course, is monitoring and assessing their efforts. See Chapter 1, Monitor Your Students' Understanding, for some suggestions on creating opportunities for assessment and feedback.

4 Remember That Learning Word Parts Is an Ongoing Process

After this discussion of the rules, patterns, and many exceptions of word building, we can understand why, in the end, using word parts is considered a creative process. That is, the learner cannot rely on predictable rules. Effective word-part learning requires a great deal of language exposure and experience over a long period of time. Gently remind students that they should expect learning word parts to be an ongoing process.

Encourage students to continue experimenting by looking for patterns and taking risks with informed guesses. Also point out that being an effective user of word parts includes the recognition of their limitations. Some words cannot be teased apart or analyzed in terms of identifiable patterns. These words are best learned as "unanalyzed wholes."[20]

ACTIVITIES

1 Word Surgery (Dividing Words into Parts)

Goal: Learners identify the meaningful parts of a list of familiar words and indicate whether they are a result of prefixing, suffixing, or compounding.

Procedure:

1. Review the information about prefixing, suffixing, and compounding with the class (See pages 79–81 of this chapter.).

2. Provide students with a list of 5–10 recently studied words. Be sure that the list contains a mix of words that are roots, compounds, prefixed, and suffixed. Try to select words that can be used to describe a general topic. (This will be useful in the Sentence-level follow-up activity, below; e.g., *impossible, carefully, workforce, beneficial,* and *rewarding* can be used to write about the topic "my dream job.")

3. Students work in pairs to divide each word into its meaningful parts. Next, they identify the parts as roots, prefixes, or suffixes. (Words with two roots are compounds.)

4. In a class discussion, students share their answers and clarify the meanings of the parts.

Sentence-level follow-up:

1. Identify a topic that is related to the words you have selected, as mentioned in Step 2, above.

2. In pairs, students write 2–3 statements about the topic, using the prefixed or suffixed words in this exercise (no compound words).

3. Each pair exchanges sentences with another pair, and restates each sentence using a different form of the target word (i.e., using a

different prefix or suffix). They should retain the main meaning of the sentences.

4. In a class discussion, focus on the changes that were made to the target words in the new sentences.

2 Practice Producing Parts[21]

Goal: Learners group context-related words by part of speech or derivational suffix.

Procedure:

1. Write a four-column chart on the board similar to the model below. The letters at the top of the chart should spell out a topic.

2. Students work in small groups and copy the chart onto a sheet of paper.

3. Each group fills in the chart with as many topic-related words as they can. Each word should begin with the letter at the top of a column and belong to the appropriate part of speech at the left. Set a time limit of about five minutes.

4. If you would like to have a contest, give one point for each appropriate word. Give an extra point for each word that no other team has listed.

5. In a class discussion, judge the appropriateness of the words the groups wrote. (Adjectives and adverbs will probably be more loosely related than nouns and verbs.) Then, talk about the similarities and differences among the suffixes within each category. Which suffixes appear most often with each part of speech?

Variations:

1. In the left column, you might limit the categories by suffix. For example, nouns ending in *-ant* / *-ent*, *-tion*, *-ous*, etc.).

2. Write a different topic, made up of 4–6 letters in the top row (e.g., sports, nature, music), adjusting the number of columns as needed.

3. Instead of writing a word in the top row, have students select four random letters that they would like to try. Then assign a topic (e.g., *computers, politics, recreation*).

	H	O	M	E
VERBS	*to hibernate*			
NOUNS			*microwave*	
ADJECTIVES				*efficient*
ADVERBS		*originally*		

3 Compound Contest

Goal: Learners use word parts to identify related compound words, and recognize variations in the written forms.

Procedure:

1. Review the information about the written forms of compounds with the class. (See pages 80–81 of this chapter.)

2. Write the following list of words on the board. Working in small groups, students write compound words which include each of the words in the list. Have students write as many words as they can. (Students should not use dictionaries at this point.)

   paper (*newspaper, wallpaper, paperback, paper clip, paperwork*)

   book

   card

   table

   work

3. Groups report their results. If you wish to have a contest, give teams one point for each appropriate word, one point for correct spelling, and one point for each word that no other team has listed. Dictionaries may be used as needed to check accuracy of answers.

4 Change Begets Change[22]

Goal: Learners observe patterns of change in pronunciation, stress, and spelling that occur when words change parts of speech.

Procedure:

1. Write charts on the board similar to the models below. Label the columns as shown.

2. Using the examples provided in each column, explain that changes can occur in pronunciation, stress, and spelling when a word's part of speech changes. (See pages 83–84 of this chapter.)

3. Work with the students to help them add recently studied words to each column of the lists on the board. Discuss the changes that occur. Point out that changes will not occur in all words.

4. Students work in pairs to add more words to each list. Discuss new words with the class.

CHANGING NOUNS TO ADJECTIVES	
Noun	**Adjective**
office	office, official
photography	

CHANGING VERBS TO NOUNS	
Verb	**Noun**
record	
recognize	

CHANGING VERBS TO NOUNS TO NAME A PERSON WHO DOES THIS ACTION	
Verb	Noun
liberate	
educate	

Sentence-level follow-up: Select a topic that fits the words you selected. Consider topics from class discussions, recent readings, high-interest current events, or campus news.

1. Write five questions about the topic, using the appropriate verb forms in the chart. Include yes/no questions and information questions (e.g., Who. . .?; What. . .?; etc.).

2. Working in pairs, students ask and answer questions (in complete sentences). Whenever possible, the answer should contain a different part of speech than the question. Each pair writes a sample question and answer on the board for class discussion and oral practice.

> **Example:**
>
> Topic: Using Technology
> Question: Did you ever record your own voice?
> Answer: Yes, my oral language teacher required me to make a recording of my pronunciation for my final grade.

5 Is the whole equal to the sum of its parts?

Goal: Learners listen to a segment of a radio or TV commercial and identify words that are made up of meaningful parts. Then they compare the meanings of the word parts to the meaning of the whole word.

Procedure:

1. Write a four-column chart on the board similar to the model below. Label the columns as shown.

2. Select an interesting current radio or TV commercial (about one minute long). As you make your selection, try to find one that includes several compound words.

3. Review the concepts of word parts with the class, reminding students of the distinctions between prefixes, suffixes, and compounds. (See pages 79–81 of this chapter.)

4. Students listen to the taped segment, and list from 5–10 words that seem important to the meaning of the content. If you are using a video, turn off the picture to help students focus.

5. Students work in pairs to compare lists and select about five words that can be divided into parts, including as many compounds as possible. You may wish to play the segment again so that students can confirm the words.

6. In a class discussion about the students' words, check the accuracy of their comprehension. Demonstrate how to use the chart, using examples from the students' lists.

7. Pairs complete the chart and discuss their answers with the class. Dictionaries may be used as needed.

TARGET WORD	WORD PARTS	MEANINGS OF THE PARTS	MEANING OF THE WORD
miraculous	*miracle + ous*	an amazing event + adj. form	something that is unexpected or amazing

6 Tell It in Reverse

Goal: Learners identify negative words that describe an opinion they hear, and then identify those words that have corresponding positive forms and those that do not.

Procedure:

1. Review the functions of negative prefixes with the class. Remind students that not all negative forms have positive counterparts, and visa versa.

2. Tell students that you are going to read them a short text of a father's opinion. Ask them to list as many words with negative prefixes as possible to describe the opinion. For example, if they hear "boring," they might write "uninteresting." If they hear "can't be counted on," they might write "undependable."

3. Read the paragraph aloud.

   I do not like the boy that my daughter wants to marry. He doesn't talk about things that are relevant. He is boring. He likes to tell stories that are in very bad taste. Also, he doesn't make sense when he is trying to make a point, and he cannot be trusted or depended upon. He is not smart, and I don't think he will be able to support my daughter. And personally, I find him very hard to get along with.

4. Working in pairs, students compare lists. Read the story again and allow pairs to add to their lists. Then have students list all of their words on the board.

5. In a class discussion of the words, focus first on accuracy of meaning and spelling. Next, identify the opposite form of each negative word and write it on the board. When the word does not have a corresponding positive form (e.g., *disgusting, disturbing*), point this out and have students come up with another word that has the same meaning.

Sentence-level follow-up:

1. Pairs work together to summarize the father's opinion, using the negative words on the board.

2. Then, say, "As we might expect, the daughter has the opposite opinion of her father. What would her paragraph look like?" Have students rewrite the father's paragraph by replacing the negative words with positive ones.

Working with Register and Other Language Variation

*As theorists we should strive to communicate
a synopsis of the fundamental dimensions of a contention
without sacrificing the basic premises of its theoretical constructs.*

That is,

"Everything should be made as simple as possible, but not simpler."
(Albert Einstein)

That is,

Keep it simple, stupid.
(Originator unknown)

BACKGROUND

Our knowledge of register is called upon nearly every time we use words. **Register** is the variation in style that allows us to use language appropriate to a given situation. It refers to differences in formality and to other stylistic changes as well. Register is what explains the contrast between the three sentences above, one suited for researchers or scholars, another for a general audience, and one for use in an informal or humorous exchange. Register choices are determined by "who is saying what to whom, when, and why."[1]

No other aspect of language is quite as important to register as vocabulary. If you have a whole group of synonyms to select from (e.g., *fatigued, drained, exhausted, tired, wiped out, pooped*), it is often register that determines your choice. You might describe yourself as fatigued to your doctor, exhausted to your coach, and wiped out or pooped to your friend. Your choice depends on the setting you are in, your purpose, and your audience.

A register is born when the language of a certain group of people incorporates specialized words and structures to meet its particular needs. Registers vary as a result of many factors, including occupations (e.g., lawyers, teachers, college students), age (e.g., children, teenagers, older adults), purpose (e.g., chatting with a friend, interviewing for a job), and relationships (e.g., friend to friend, employer to employee). Register and language variations accomplish various purposes: they allow those within a group to express ideas that are useful to them, and they confirm membership in the group. That is, if you can understand and use the terminology of a language community, you "belong."

Educators and linguists sometimes refer to **formal register** and **informal register.** When you are explaining the concept of register, this is a good place to start, but it doesn't capture some of the subtleties of language variety that are especially difficult for learners. For example, a particular setting may not be clearly formal or informal. How is a learner to interpret a classroom in which the professor wears blue jeans and greets the class with "Hey, how's it going?" but rewards students who use academic register in class discussions and demands academic English in writing assignments? Indeed, the parameters of formality are not always straightforward. This was demonstrated by the learner who knew that academic writing requires a formal register and that the word *guts* is informal. Unaware that some idioms are fixed, she sought to formalize an informal expression:

> *He spilled his intestines to his therapist.

Another cause of confusion is the fact that the use of formal or informal words in English isn't determined only by particular settings or relationships. The choice often carries a subtle meaning that the user intends to convey. For example, we might use a casual style with a stranger to put the person at ease. Similarly, we may choose a more formal style, even with friends or family, when we want to establish some distance or express a position of power.

Although register is a feature of every known language, language learners often aren't conscious of the factors that affect register in a new language. They aren't aware of which word choices, made for one purpose or audience, will not sound "normal" for another. Some of the most common errors non-proficient speakers of a language make relate to mixing words from different registers and other inappropriate register choices.2

Alertness to register is empowering. An understanding of the subtleties of register gives us great flexibility with self expression, enabling us to express ourselves with skill and confidence in a variety of settings.

A CLOSER LOOK AT REGISTER AND LANGUAGE VARIATION

1 Spoken and Written Registers

Written language is normally more formal than spoken language.[3] It is characterized by precise, non-conversational vocabulary (e.g., *rancid* instead of *spoiled; thrifty* instead of *cheap*). The precise and accurate use of vocabulary, as well as grammar, is more important in writing than in everyday conversation, in part because writing is not supplemented with gesture, facial expression, tone of voice, and the other ways we express ourselves in person. Standard spoken English tends to be casual and interactive, depending largely on give and take with one's conversational partner.

Learners don't always recognize the distinction between spoken and written registers. When learners use written-language vocabulary in conversation, they often sound opinionated or stilted. On the other hand, when a student's academic writing includes informal words, such as *guys* or *kids*, it might be due to the influence of spoken language. An error like this, however, may be interpreted as inappropriate or even "uneducated" language. Students need to learn that many informal words, used frequently in spoken language, should be avoided in writing. Here is a sampling of those:

INFORMAL OR COLLOQUIAL WORDS (USED IN SPEECH)	FORMAL COUNTERPARTS (USED IN WRITING)
a lot (*alot* is not a word)	many, several, numerous, a great number, a large amount
all right (sometimes spelled *alright*)	fine, acceptable
get (to obtain)	obtain, find, acquire, retrieve
get (to understand)	understand, comprehend
for sure	I am sure; I am positive; I know for certain
gonna	going to
How come?	Why?
kid (to joke)	joke, tease
kind of, sort of (*kinda* and *sorta* are not words)	somewhat, rather
let	allow, permit

2 Academic Register

Academic English is formal English that is specially suited for academic or educational purposes. It typically serves language functions that are needed by students and teachers in high schools, colleges, and universities, as well as scholars and researchers. Academic English requires high levels of competency with many linguistic features and with a large, specifically academic vocabulary.[4]

Choosing the most important academic words for your students should depend on their needs. For example, some teachers consider English words of Greek and Latin origin to be the most important.[5] Others select words needed in the classroom (e.g., *define, abbreviate, speculate, viewpoint*).[6] Sometimes, teachers use lists of words that are identified through word frequency counts of academic materials.[7] Whatever the nature of the particular list, learners can't simply "pick up" academic vocabulary because it is generally rare in everyday conversation; thus, learners have less exposure to it.[8]

Mastery of the academic register in general, and academic vocabulary in particular, is absolutely necessary for school success. Without it, learners don't have access to the content of the school curriculum. They can't understand what they read, participate in discussions, or complete written assignments. It has been claimed that without academic vocabulary, learners are "hindered in their oral and written language and perhaps in their thinking as well."[9]

3 Spoken and Colloquial Registers

Language formality / informality is best described as a continuum rather than as two distinct categories. This is especially apparent in spoken English, which ranges from the more formal standard spoken English (found in a given community's media, dictionaries, and schools) to the more informal colloquial English (used in everyday situations). The distinction between formal and colloquial speech is often blurred and ultimately decided by each speech community.

As spoken English becomes less formal, it tends to be faster and more casual. It tends to use more phrasal verbs (e.g., *fill in for* instead of *replace*; *put in* instead of *insert*). It contains more reduced forms (e.g., *wanna* and *gonna* rather than *want to* and *going to*), more chatty or casual words and phrases (e.g., *ok, no problem, sure*), and more idioms. In colloquial English, there is more use of name-calling (e.g., *He's a fool!* rather than *He's foolish.*), hyperbole (e.g., *I asked him millions of times.*), "sound effects" (e.g., *Yuk! Wow!*), and slang (*Did you see the size of that rock?* rather than *Did you notice the size of that diamond?*).

4 Slang

Slang is not new; Shakespeare was well known for choosing such terms as *clay-brained* and *clod-pole* over *stupid* or *unintelligent*. Over time slang words are often accepted into the mainstream; the terms *phone* and *bike* were once considered slang, but are now standard terms. Slang appears in many registers, but is most common in colloquial language. Slang words are usually associated with a particular social, geographical, or age group, and stem from a desire to make language vivid, new, and colorful. The words range from casual to crude and they appear as various parts of speech (e.g., *nerd, nifty, to nuke*).

One of the challenges posed by slang words is that they move in and out of style quickly: something good was described as keen in the 1950s, *groovy* or *far out* in the 1960s, then as *cool, awesome, sweet,* or *tight* more recently.[10] Another challenge is that some words have one meaning in general use and a very different meaning as slang. For example, the word *hot* (opposite of cold) has been used in slang to mean "urgent," "stolen," "performing well," "angry," "sexy," and "popular."[11] The same problem with multiple meanings applies to many other words, such as *bad* (which can be slang for *good*) and *stupid* (which can be slang for "great" or "a large amount").

Each group of speakers judges for itself what is standard spoken English and what is colloquial, and these judgments can change. This is one of many ways that language is constantly in flux. There is no shortcut to understanding the register choices of the many groups your students will encounter. Encourage them to pay attention to who uses which words when, and then to follow the lead of the people they wish to emulate.

5 Other Types of Register and Language Variation

Register and other types of language variation is generally a reflection of a person's social roles, social position, or social relationships. The language used by a person in authority, or with someone you want to impress, is normally more formal and more distant than the language you use with a friend (e.g., *acquire* rather than *get, converse* rather than *chat*). The language of power tends to be formal and indirect (e.g., *Your compensation is commensurate with your performance.*), rather than familiar and empathetic (e.g., *If you work hard, we will make it worth your effort.*). In almost every situation, word choice is directly related to power relations, prestige, and politeness.

Euphemism

One way that people express politeness or use discretion is through the use of **euphemisms**: words or phrases used in place of terms considered too direct, offensive, or unpleasant. Euphemisms allow us to neutralize or distance ourselves from topics that make us uncomfortable, such as death (e.g., *He's no longer with us.*), physiological functions (e.g., *I need to visit the ladies room.*), or sex (e.g., *It isn't right for professors to sleep with their students.*).

Euphemisms are also used to soften or neutralize topics that are morally or ethically sensitive (e.g., prostitutes are *comfort women* or *ladies of the night*) or impolite (e.g., a large person is *big-boned* or *amply proportioned*; a disabled person is *physically challenged*). Euphemisms can vary in formality and connotation. Instead of *die*, for example, the word *expire* is more formal and dispassionate than *pass away*. (Phrases like *bite the dust* or *cash in your chips* are even more informal and have humorous connotations.) Learners who don't recognize the subtle suggestions expressed in euphemisms are at a disadvantage both in their comprehension of others and in their self-expression.

Domain-specific vocabulary and jargon

Language variations also occur within different domains of use, such as occupations and fields of interest. In the same way that formal and informal registers are a continuum, so, too, are domain-specific vocabulary and jargon. **Domain-specific vocabulary** usually refers to common words used in a particular way in the context of a domain. These words can be challenging because they may have different meanings depending on whether they are used in a specific register or in common usage. In everyday language, *normal* means "ordinary" or "usual." In engineering, however, *normal* refers to something that is perpendicular to a surface.

In the area of technology, some commonly used words have been assigned new meanings (e.g., *web, real estate, virus, import*), and others have changed parts of speech (e.g., *access* and *key* were used only as nouns before the computer industry introduced them as verbs[12]).

Many professions and interest areas have register distinctions that characterize their language use from that of other groups. Think for a moment of an interest area of yours. Chances are you use common words in particular ways in the context of that interest area that would make them not immediately understandable to someone unfamiliar with it, regardless of English proficiency. For example, garden enthusiasts speak of planting *annuals*, and at the end of a *play* baseball players toss the ball *around the horn*.

Jargon refers to specialized words from one field or occupation that are not easily understood by outsiders. These are specialty words that are precisely designed for the needs of a given field and not usually used with the same meaning outside of that domain. For example, fashion designers use *knitdown* (a fabric sample sent to a factory for evaluation of a sweater stitch); brokers talk about *achieving liquidity* (when one has access to cash), and chat room users might begin a session with *HT* ("Hi, there.") and end with *L8R* ("Later.") or *BFN* ("Bye for now.").

Jargon allows those within a field to talk about abstract or central ideas in shorthand, and it confirms membership to the group. If you don't understand the terminology, you can't participate in the conversation. Jargon is a necessary tool for precise and specialized expression within a field. When too much jargon is used at one time, excluding "outsiders" from participation, it can be perceived negatively as *lawyerese, business-speak, teacher-talk*, etc.

People's responses to jargon tell us something about word learning that we can apply to our teaching. That is, when we don't know a word that is comfortably used by a certain group, we may feel that we don't belong. Similarly, many of our learners feel like outsiders when they don't understand the vocabulary being used, and they may be reluctant to ask for the meanings they don't know. We can help them by encouraging questions and creating a supportive learning environment.

6 Register and Sociocultural Knowledge Are Intertwined

Understanding register requires understanding a given community's socially defined relationships. A register cannot be separated from the situation in which it is used. That's why we can't rely on textbooks alone to teach students about register and language variation. Whatever happens inside the classroom needs to be fully informed by the reality of the outside world. Authenticity is critical.

Authenticity of content

Registers and language varieties are constantly in flux, as are the roles of the people who use them. Words move from one register to another, often changing meaning. New words enter the language all the time. Roles between participants change, influencing the formality and informality of their interactions. Learners must come to recognize language as a social activity rather than a collection of rules to follow. Encourage your students to participate in observations, interviews, service learning assignments, action research assignments, and other activities that allow them to interact with authentic language. These types of experiences will help learners become more aware of the social nature of language.

Authenticity of learner roles

It is a great disservice to learners to focus only on their role as student. In reality, learners have many social identities (e.g., parent, consumer, employee / employer, etc.). Allow them to observe and participate in the language used by groups that share these other identities.[13] Be careful not to limit tasks to those that are defined and constrained by the classroom.

Authenticity of language practice

Authentic practice occurs when a language activity is intrinsically motivating and offers participants a chance to freely and naturally express themselves.[14] For example, if you brought a newspaper article to class, an authentic activity would be to elicit your students' opinions about the topic of the article. It would not be authentic to have them memorize the article or conjugate its verbs, for example. It is also important to have students practice language forms that fit the context of the lesson (e.g., Does your lesson about making a dental appointment elicit the actual language used for this task?).

You can provide authentic practice in a controlled environment like the classroom. Ultimately, however, for learners to acquire a particular register, they will need exposure to and interaction with the real language community that uses it.

KEY CONSIDERATIONS FOR THE CLASSROOM

1 Consider Register When Choosing Target Words

There are many words that are neutral, or used in all registers. These words are easier to learn because they don't require the knowledge of complex social relationships. Learners need a lot of exposure to neutral words. It is also helpful to talk about new words in terms of their usefulness. If a word is specific to a certain domain or level of formality, let students know, and encourage them to seek that kind of information about new words on their own.

Acquaint learners with words in registers related to their goals and interests. Guide them in individual word-learning activities (e.g., word learning logs, observation assignments, etc.) that will result in lists of new words tailored to their needs. See Chapter 7 for further discussion of individual word learning.

2 Be Aware of Register Differences Between Languages

Learners will encounter some new words in English with similar forms and meanings in their first language; however, these words may be used in different registers. For example, the word *profound* in English is a relatively formal word used in a fairly restricted realm (e.g., *profound ideas; profound revelation*). In Spanish, the corresponding word, *profundo*, has a more general use and can refer to anything that is deep, such as a lake. Similarly, *petition* in English is used for a specific and relatively limited type of formal request; in Spanish, *petición* is an informal noun used for any request. Calling attention to the fact that there are register differences when you present new words will help your students identify these differences on their own, giving them the insight to use the word appropriately in English.

3 Expect the Learning of Register to Be Ongoing

It takes a long time to acquire an understanding of register and language variation. It is a gradual process that requires a great deal of experience with language. Learners will benefit from interactive activities that highlight features, such as degrees of formality, slang, domain-specific registers, and other factors that influence word choice.

Students also need to learn how to be independent learners of register. They need to ask the right questions about new words and to seek useful information about who uses a word, when it is used, and why. Finally, as independent learners, students need to have efficient dictionary skills that will help them access relevant information. For example, the list below includes many of the features of register mentioned in this chapter. Consult the dictionaries most often used by your students. With your students, review the terms and abbreviations they will encounter while using them. See Chapter 7 for further information about dictionary skills.

TERM	COMMON NOTATIONS REGARDING REGISTER
American English	US
archaic; obsolete; old-fashioned	archaic; obs; old fashioned; old use
Biblical	Bibl
British English	Bre; Brit
dialect; dialectal	dial
euphemistic	euph
feminine	fem
formal	fml
informal	infml
literary	literary
offensive	offensive
pompous	pomp
slang	slang
technical	technical
taboo	tabuu

ACTIVITIES

1 Newsworthy Words

Goal: Learners identify words that are associated with a specific domain and register.

Procedure:

1. Divide the class into small groups, and give each group a different section of a newspaper (or direct them to use a different section of an online news site), such as sports, business, entertainment, or international news.

2. Groups select one article and scan it quickly. Tell students to select short articles when possible or to read about 4–6 paragraphs of longer articles.

3. Students work together to identify a list of 5–10 words that represent the domain and reflect the register of the article and/or represent its main point. For example, a business article on a new marketing strategy might contain *promote, sales, revenue, marketing, emerging market,* and *customers.*

4. Groups exchange lists without looking at each other's articles and answer the following questions:
   a. Which section do you think the article was in?
   b. What do you think the topic of the article is?
   c. What do you think the main point or gist of the article is? (if possible)

5. In a class discussion, talk about the similarities and differences of the target words in each domain. You may want to write each set of domain-specific words on the board to facilitate the discussion and prepare for the sentence-level follow-up.

Sentence-level follow-up:

1. Assign each student a partner from a different group—someone who read about sports might work with someone who read about business.

2. Students take turns asking questions about the article they didn't read, using a domain-appropriate target word in each question. Since the students haven't had time to gain a thorough understanding of the articles, their answers will most likely be general. For example:

> Question: What product is this company trying to <u>promote?</u>
>
> Answer: I'm not sure, but they are <u>marketing</u> it to a lot of customers.

2 Computer Components[15]

Goal: Learners analyze words from the computer technology domain, and discuss how the words were formed.

Procedure:

1. Write the following words on the board: download, gigabyte, migrate, mouse, broadband, domain name, Ethernet, chat room, motherboard. Add additional words if you wish.

2. Students work in pairs to identify the words as one of these types:
   a. compounds based on familiar words (motherboard)
   b. words borrowed from another domain (mouse)
   c. entirely new words (gigabyte)

3. In a class discussion, focus on the ways in which the word parts or the original meaning of the words are related to the new words. That is, consider how the words in the list were formed.

3 Euphemistic Expression

Goal: Learners identify euphemisms and discuss their meanings.

Procedure:

1. Write all or some of the following on the board: *die, toilet, drunk, insane, fat, old person.*

2. Pairs list as many euphemisms as they can for each of the words.

3. In a class discussion, compare the differences in meaning among the euphemisms. Draw attention to the differences in connotation, formality, and the situations in which the different euphemisms might be used.

Sentence-level follow-up:

Students work in pairs to write a personal ad for a dating service. They should describe themselves or an imaginary person using euphemisms for physical and personality characteristics. You can determine how many euphemisms they should use or simply tell them to use as many as they can.

4 Register Transformations: Coworker Complaint

Goal: Learners identify the key words that distinguish an informal email from a more formal message.

Procedure:

1. Review with the class the information about written, spoken, and colloquial registers. Also review how to use dictionary abbreviations to identify the formality of a word (See page 104 of this chapter.).

2. Hand out the following email message from one coworker to another or write it on the board (or create a similar email of your own). Have the class read the email together. Clarify the meanings of unfamiliar words.

3. Students work in pairs to underline the informal or colloquial words in the message. For each underlined item, they should identify more formal counterparts. Dictionaries may be used as needed.

4. In a class discussion, students compare the various words in the message and discuss formal counterparts for each one.

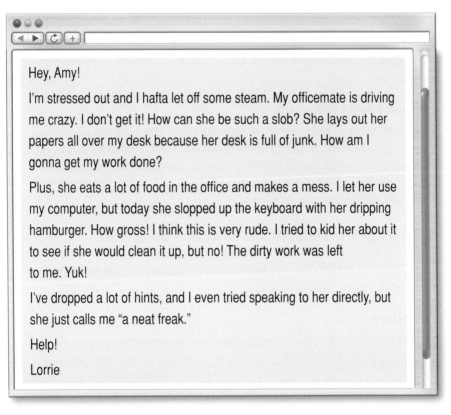

Hey, Amy!

I'm stressed out and I hafta let off some steam. My officemate is driving me crazy. I don't get it! How can she be such a slob? She lays out her papers all over my desk because her desk is full of junk. How am I gonna get my work done?

Plus, she eats a lot of food in the office and makes a mess. I let her use my computer, but today she slopped up the keyboard with her dripping hamburger. How gross! I think this is very rude. I tried to kid her about it to see if she would clean it up, but no! The dirty work was left to me. Yuk!

I've dropped a lot of hints, and I even tried speaking to her directly, but she just calls me "a neat freak."

Help!

Lorrie

Sentence-level follow-up:

Pairs rewrite the email, expressing the same complaints to a supervisor. They must use an appropriate register and keep the content as similar as possible.

5 Words at Work

Goal: Learners identify words that are commonly used within one familiar domain and one that is unfamiliar.

Procedure:

1. Review with the class the information about domain-specific vocabulary and jargon (See pages 100–102 of this chapter.).

2. Group learners according to their future goals or majors (e.g., business, science, architecture, etc.). For those who are undecided

about their majors, select another area of interest or familiarity (e.g., politics, sports, restaurant work, childcare, etc.).

3. Each group brainstorms a list of ten or more words that are used in the group's chosen field. Then they identify the words that they consider to be jargon. Dictionaries may be used as needed.

4. Groups discuss their lists, asking and answering questions (e.g., *Which of these words are used most often? Which are most difficult for others to understand?*). Then, groups select five words that they consider most important to someone working in their field.

5. Regroup students into pairs so that each one has a partner from a different field. Learners explain the five words to their partners, focusing on when they would be used and by whom.

Sentence-level follow-up:
Students write 2–3 questions about the field they heard about (#4, above), using one example of jargon in each question.

> **Example**
>
> How much money did your project team spend on signage when you promoted this project?

6 Tactful or Tricky?[16]

Goal: Learners identify the differences in meaning and register of a pair of near-synonyms and indicate when and why they might use each one.

Procedure:
1. Write the following word pairs on the board:
   a. lying/prevaricating
   b. partly cloudy/partly sunny
   c. a nightspot/a club
   d. free enterprise/capitalism
   e. recession/a business slump
   f. a handicapped person/a cripple

2. Students work in pairs to identify the differences between the word pairs and describe a circumstance (including the place and the audience) in which they would use each item.

3. Have a class discussion about the students' observations. When possible, students should identify the register in which each word might occur.

   Example

   A news report about a trial would use a more formal register. The newscaster might report that a witness was "prevaricating" rather than lying.

4. Brainstorm additional word pairs with the class. Discuss the differences.

7 Formal Counterparts

Goal: Learners identify formal counterparts for informal or colloquial words.

Procedure:

1. Review the information with the class about informal / colloquial and formal language and the value of learner dictionaries in this regard. Remember that it's sometimes hard to distinguish between informal words and colloquial words; treat them as one category for this exercise. (See pages 98–99 and 104 of this chapter.)

2. Write a list of informal / colloquial words on the board. Use your own words or the ones suggested below.

3. Pronounce the words for the students. Discuss meanings as needed.

4. Students work in pairs to identify formal counterparts for each word. First, they do the task without dictionaries. Then, they do it again, this time using dictionaries or thesauruses.

5. Have a class discussion about the students' lists. Check for accuracy and variety.

INFORMAL OR COLLOQUIAL WORDS	FORMAL COUNTERPARTS
ok or okay	*fine, acceptable*
could of, would of, should of	
cute	
wanna	
kid (a young person)	
cheap (an adjective to describe a person)	
haggle	
kind of, sort of (*kinda* and *sorta* are not words)	
snoop	

Sentence-level follow-up:

Tell students to imagine that they are on vacation in a place of their choice.

1. Students work in pairs to write a postcard note (or short email) to a friend, telling them about their vacation. They should use 3–5 of the colloquial words from the class list.

2. Then, pairs work together to write the equivalent message to their boss, using 3–5 of the formal counterparts.

8 Slang Survey

Goal: Learners analyze and compare the slang used by proficient speakers of English from different age groups.

Procedure:

1. This activity will work well as homework or as an off-campus activity. It is best if students work in pairs, but they can work alone if that is more practical.

2. Provide guidelines for students to conduct oral interviews with proficient speakers of English. Students write the following words in their notebooks: *girl, boy, good, bad, stupid.*

3. Each pair or individual chooses a proficient English speaker to interview. Try to have as much variety in the ages of the interviewees as possible. (Across the whole class, the interviewees should include at least one child, teenager, college student, and older adult.)

4. Students will ask each informant to provide as many slang words as possible for each of the words listed in #2 above.

5. In a class discussion, have students compare lists, focusing on the similarities and differences between people of different ages. Ask students to consider what other factors (besides age) might influence the slang used by different people.

Helping Students Become Independent Word Learners

There are things, in an unknown place, that you won't know how to look for, shapes you won't recognize, movement you won't understand. Learning the language of a landscape is the way we come to inhabit our world.

(From a travel magazine about New Zealand, cited by Leo van Lier[1])

BACKGROUND

Like a hiker who is trying to make sense of a new landscape, learners know that the secrets of a new word are hidden in the details of its surroundings, its purpose, and its form. When you see or hear a new word, there are many ways to learn about it. Ask yourself questions, such as *Who said the word? Where was it used,* and *Why?* The answers will provide hints about the word's meaning, connotations, formality, and register. You can also apply your background knowledge by asking questions like *Do I know any of the word parts? Do the surrounding sentences shed light on the meaning? Do certain words co-occur with this word? Are there grammatical patterns that the word requires?* Effective learners know how to go about gathering information about a new word with each encounter.

Word learning is incremental; the process continues long after we meet a word for the first time. Even after we feel confident using a word, there are often gaps in our knowledge. For example, a Vietnamese university student studying in the United States commented to his male friend, "Your shirt is darling." His friend was appalled and the student was embarrassed. He had studied English for many years in Vietnam and felt confident that he understood the meaning and use of *darling.* He had never noticed (or been told) that this word is usually used by women. This is an example of partial word knowledge; the student knew nearly everything he needed to know about using the word *darling* except one very significant detail. Learners can pick up fine points of word knowledge such as this by sharpening their observation skills, by not being afraid to make mistakes, and by understanding that word learning is a gradual process.

Students learn only a fraction of the words they need in the classroom, and they often have only partial knowledge of the ones they learn. Therefore, teaching students to be independent word learners is critical. This begins with an understanding of what it means to know a word and the ability to notice what is important. It continues with a working knowledge of word-learning strategies and the ability to use those strategies selectively. In fact, students cannot be truly independent as word learners until they can use strategies well. We can facilitate such independence by teaching, modeling, and practicing the ways to approach new vocabulary that will enable our students to be successful in the lifelong process of word learning. As the old saying goes, "Give a man a fish and feed him for a day; teach a man to fish and feed him for a lifetime."

A CLOSER LOOK AT INDEPENDENT WORD LEARNING

1 Understanding the Word Learning Task

An understanding of what it means to know a word can serve as a framework for the learner. As we have seen throughout this book, knowing a word means knowing about its many aspects: its meaning(s), collocations, grammatical behavior, derivations, and register. Within each of these categories there are many details that can guide a learner's observations and questions. For example, understanding the concept of collocation can help a learner be more alert to fixed phrases or to words that always occur with the same preposition. Without this awareness, knowledge is only partial, and as we have seen, partial knowledge of a word often leads to errors.

ASPECT OF WORD KNOWLEDGE	EXAMPLE OF PARTIAL KNOWLEDGE	EXPLANATION OF PARTIAL KNOWLEDGE
Meaning	From a brochure advertising holiday specials at a luxury hotel in Bratislava, Slovakia: *"New Year's Eve for the demanding!"	The intended meaning here is "discriminating." Although discriminating people may also be demanding, the words are not synonyms. (Note: Errors like this sometimes occur when learners' information is limited to bilingual dictionaries or thesauruses.)
Collocation	*"It comes without speaking that I would want to understand my heritage."	The learner appears to know the meaning of the idiom *it goes without saying,* but doesn't know the appropriate collocations in the fixed phrase.
Grammatical features	*"We were frightening when our car began to skid out of control."	The learner doesn't know that expressing the appropriate meaning for this sentence requires the past participle *frightened,* not the present participle, *frightening.*
Word parts	*"This is my professional."	The student is using the right word family, but has chosen the adjective form rather than the required noun form.
Register	Prospective employee at a job interview: *"At my last job I bagged a good deal for the company and brought in over a million bucks."	The content is appropriate for an interview, but *bagged, good deal* and *bucks* are colloquial; they would be suitable for bragging about the accomplishment to a good friend, not a prospective employer.

2 Word Learning Strategies

Word learning strategies are important because they enable students to take responsibility for their learning and to direct their own efforts. Some strategies guide learners' thoughts and questions about words;

others focus their attention as they listen, read, or participate in conversation. The most effective learning takes place when students know a variety of strategies that serve different purposes.

Reflection

Perceptive learners are able to accurately assess their own understanding of a new word, and then to reflect on the information that will lead them to using that word appropriately. The savvy learner focuses on the features of a word that seem especially important for effective use. Both understand that word knowledge doesn't happen all at once.

We don't just "know" or "not know" a word; we are always at varying stages of knowledge for each word we are learning. For example, there are some words that we avoid using in writing because we are unsure of the spelling. There are some nouns that we use with caution because we are unsure of their countability. There are still other words that we can roughly understand in context, but are unwilling to use in our own expression.

One way to guide learners' self-assessment is to show them how to evaluate their knowledge of each new word with a scale like this:[2]

I have never seen the word before.	I have seen the word but am not sure what it means.	I under-stand the word when I see or hear it in a sentence.	I have tried to use this word, but I am not sure I am using it correctly.	I use the word with confidence in either speaking *or* writing.	I use the word with confidence, both in speaking *and* writing.

The self-assessment exercise reminds learners of the incremental nature of word learning and helps them focus on areas needing practice. If students do the exercise both before and after a word is practiced in class, it can also be an indicator of the effectiveness of the lesson.

Students can also aid their word learning by reflecting on the roles and purposes of the people who use a word. This type of examination can provide insights about a word's meaning, formality, register, age- and setting-appropriateness, and more. Alert observers can take this further and pick up variations in meaning and register of partially known words by noticing how the words are used in different contexts. For example, the verb *digest* has one meaning in the lunch room (e.g., *I find cheese difficult to digest.*) and another meaning in a classroom (e.g., *The professor's conclusions were difficult to digest.*). It can have a slightly different meaning in other settings (e.g., *I waited while she tried to digest the bad news.*). The learner who knows the first meaning can use that information, along with the new contexts, and probably figure out the second two.

In addition to directing our students to observe language use in different contexts, it is important that we also encourage them to notice how people respond to their use of words. (Consider the example above of the student who used *darling* inappropriately.)

Asking questions about words

Teachers often value good questions more than students do; we know that the best students are often the ones who are alert to pertinent details and who are willing to ask about them. When learners understand what it means to know a word, they have what they need to formulate intelligent, productive questions. And we must encourage them to do so!

Questions should dig much deeper than "What does the word mean?" or "What is a good synonym?" An effective learner will ask questions like these:

■ Are there certain words that often occur before or after the word? (collocation)

■ (If it's a verb) Is there any particular preposition that often follows it? (collocation)

■ Are there any grammatical patterns that occur with the word? (grammar)

■ (If it's a noun) Is it countable or uncountable? (grammar)

■ Are there any familiar roots or affixes for this word? (word parts)

■ Did we study any other members of this word family? (word parts)

■ Is the word used by both men and women? (register / appropriateness)

■ Is the word used in both speaking and writing? (register / appropriateness)

■ Could this word be used to refer to people? Animals? Things? (meaning)

■ Does the word have any positive or negative connotations? (meaning)

Using context

Although context can provide a great deal of meaning for the reader, we can't assume that it will always be helpful. In order for readers to be able to guess words in context, they must know 95% of the words in the text[3]; that is, 19 out of 20 words. Even this percentage of knowledge can cause difficulty; in fact, 98% (one unknown word in 50) is considered an "independent reading level."[4]

Likewise, context clues can be unusable, incomplete, or nonexistent. Research shows that incorrect guesses are more frequent than correct ones, and that the most common way people deal with unfamiliar words in reading is by ignoring them.[5] It is therefore unwise for us, as teachers, to overestimate the effectiveness or ease of "just guessing." We must be aware of both the limitations of context and also the characteristics of helpful context clues.

Limitations of context: Context is not always an adequate provider of meaning because clues are often partial, and sometimes there are no clues at all. It's also important to remember that cultural and linguistic barriers often make guessing from context difficult. In addition, research has shown that local clues lead to more accurate guesses than global clues. That is, it's easier to make guesses about meaning when a clue is located near an unknown word. It's more difficult when the clue requires an integrated understanding of the text beyond the sentence in which the word appears.[6]

Consider the role of context as you try to guess the meanings of the words in this example. Notice that, as a proficient reader, you can probably make reasonable choices that make sense; guessing the exact word is more difficult.

> A nonprofit organization called *Helping Hands* works to accommodate the needs of (1) _____. This (2) _____ group trains small monkeys so they can meet the daily needs of severely disabled people. A monkey named Jo, for example, is trained to bring books or magazines, clear away empty glasses, and pick up dropped items. She is able to respond to spoken commands such as "bring" or "change." Her owner, who is confined to a wheelchair, admits that there are occasional misunderstandings, but, overall, she is worth her weight in (3) _____.[7]

TARGET WORD	LIMITATION OF CONTEXT CLUE
1. quadriplegic	**Global clue:** The meaning isn't clear until the last sentence of the paragraph. The clue is also partial; it refers to anyone who uses a wheelchair, not just one who is quadriplegic.
2. innovative	**Partial clue:** The examples in the text suggest innovativeness, but they equally suggest other descriptions with very different meanings: *generous, helpful, philanthropic,* etc.
3. gold	**Linguistic / cultural clue:** The knowledge of the idiom *worth one's weight in gold* is needed to understand this otherwise confusing tangent about the monkey's weight. Linguistic and cultural knowledge is also needed to understand the meaning of (and use) *nonprofit organization*.

Characteristics of helpful context clues: Some context clues can be helpful in reading comprehension but not necessarily adequate for word learning. As shown in the exercise, clues often facilitate the understanding of a text, but they don't provide enough information to guess (and learn) the exact meaning of the words. Most texts do not define words; they rely on the inference skills of the reader.

In fact, there is debate over whether it is a good use of valuable class time to teach specific types of context clues at all. Some educators argue that students benefit more from practice that uses context and focuses on comprehension rather than on identifying specific types of clues[8] (e.g., synonyms or restatements, comparisons or contrasts, examples, direct explanations, summaries, etc.).

As you discuss context clues in class, think about the nature of the clues you encounter in authentic texts: those that are most valuable tend to help you make inferences about the text.

Using word parts

Chapter 5 of this book discusses the use of word parts in some detail; the topic is included here because a list of word learning strategies would not be complete without it. Breaking words into meaningful parts facilitates decoding by a reader / listener and the word-building of a speaker / writer. One of the challenges is to know when a word can be dissembled into meaningful parts (e.g., *bake + er = baker*) and when it cannot (e.g., *father, shoulder*). Learners need to recognize that word parts can be both a resource and an obstacle.

3 Using the Dictionary

For many language learners, the dictionary is an underused resource. In fact, efficient and fruitful dictionary use is more challenging than it might at first appear. As teachers, we can help by taking time to examine dictionaries on our own and thinking about the challenges they pose. Guidance with dictionary selection, and guided practice with dictionary use, will serve learners well.

Dictionary selection

Effective dictionary use begins with choosing an appropriate dictionary. Students will ultimately select their own dictionaries, but you can help them make good choices by pointing out what is most important.

Date: Dictionaries need to be up-to-date. Over time, familiar words change meanings, parts of speech, and more (e.g., *logistics* was once used only to refer to military details and organization; *access* was formerly identified as a noun, not both a noun and a verb). About 1,000 new words are added to English each year.[9] A good rule of thumb is to replace dictionaries that are more than ten years old.

Purpose: Ask students to consider the purpose for which they will use their dictionaries. Their purposes should influence their choices. The term **learner dictionary** is used to distinguish those designed specifically for second or foreign language learners. These provide additional grammatical and cultural information that will address the particular questions of the language learner (e.g., whether a noun is countable or uncountable). Some learner dictionaries are designed for the beginning student. These feature definitions and sample sentences that require knowledge of as few as 2,000 words to understand. Other dictionaries are geared toward advanced learners. They contain more entries, more information, and more academic content. And there is no limit to the wide variety of specialized dictionaries. They can range from accounting to etymology, from idioms to medicine, from slang to wine.

Clarity: Some dictionaries offer clearer definitions, sample sentences, and grammatical explanations than other dictionaries. Point out to students that definitions should be direct and clear and that sample sentences should reflect natural usage along with features like collocations and register. For example, in one dictionary, the definition of *God* is quite complicated: "the supreme Deity and self-existent Creator and Upholder of the universe." (No sample sentence is offered.) Another dictionary defines *God* more directly and with more familiar vocabulary: "In Christianity, Islam and Judaism, the creator and ruler of all things." Three sample sentences are provided, including, "Dear God, please help us."

The symbols used also need to be clear. Show students how to recognize the notations for useful grammatical information such as countable / uncountable nouns, irregular verb forms, objects of phrasal verbs, and so on.

You can facilitate effective dictionary selection by taking class time to expose your students to a variety of dictionaries and to compare them according to age, purpose, and clarity. In a class discussion, read several entries for the same target word and talk about the clarity of the definition and the role of the sample sentences (if any). Look up words such as *God, profit* (noun), and *free market* and compare the differences. Have a variety of dictionaries on hand, including old dictionaries, electronic dictionaries, and bilingual dictionaries. Through a clear demonstration of the contrasts, you can enable learners to make their own choices about the best dictionary for them.

Selective use of the dictionary

Although effective dictionary use can facilitate learner independence, overuse of the dictionary causes problems. Dictionary users can focus too much on the definition of a word in isolation and overlook the context or the word-part clues.

Encourage your students to be selective about when and how they use their dictionaries. Before they look up a word, teach students to ask themselves the following questions to decide whether the dictionary is truly needed:

1. Do I need the word? Can I understand the text without it? Is it a word I may find valuable later?

2. Does the context help?

3. Do the word parts help?

4. Does it help to pronounce it? Does it sound like a word that I know?

It's easy to take dictionary use for granted, but overuse of the dictionary can also interrupt the flow of concentration. Consider the mental tasks involved with looking up any word:

■ using an alphabetic list;

■ removing affixes, if necessary, to identify the base form of the word;

■ using the context to decide which part of speech is needed; and

■ using the context to decide which meaning is appropriate.[10]

We can facilitate efficient dictionary use by isolating these skills and providing guided practice in class. For example, you can easily design a class activity or game that practices finding words in an alphabetical list, removing suffixes, or identifying parts of speech of words in context.

Dealing with definitions

If a dictionary definition is not clear and immediately useful, most of us will gloss over it. In fact, using a dictionary requires considerable patience and some familiarity with the characteristics of definitions.

Many definitions begin with a **classifier**, or a more general category (e.g., A car is a vehicle . . .) and continue with **distinguishers**, the details needed to distinguish the word from others in its category (e.g., A car is a vehicle with an engine and four wheels that up to six people can ride in.). These details distinguish a car from a bicycle ("a vehicle with two wheels that you sit on and ride by moving your legs"). Some classifiers are not single words, but small phrases (e.g., a field is an area of land…). The distinguisher information does not always occur at the end of the sentence (e.g., A carrot is a long, thin, orange vegetable that grows underground.).

To provide practice in recognizing classifiers and distinguishers, have your students compare how different dictionaries define the following word groups:

- bus, van, truck, motorcycle

- carrot, cucumber, broccoli, cabbage, tomato[11]

Definitions alone don't give much information about how words are used, and, in fact, they can lead to learner errors. Good learner dictionaries provide information beyond the definition (e.g., collocations and sample sentences), information which can help students avoid errors. Advise learners to look at all the information the dictionary provides, not just the definition.

Definitions can be difficult for many reasons. They sometimes use unfamiliar words, incomplete sentences, and/or abbreviations that can seem cryptic to the learner. You can best address these problems through modeling, discussion, and guided practice. Keep a dictionary on hand as you teach and frequently demonstrate the process of looking up an unfamiliar word and navigating the definition. Model the characteristics of effective definition use:

1. Before looking up the unknown word, think carefully about the context in which you find the word.

2. Since many words have several meanings, read all of them before you decide which one fits your need.

3. Be sure to read all parts of the definition.

Students need the idea reinforced that the dictionary works best when you use it in combination with the context and what you know about word parts. They need to consider all of these sources as they decide upon the meaning of a word.

4 Memory Aids

All word learners need a way to pursue self-selected words at their own pace. Practice using a variety of techniques for this in class and encourage learners to adopt the ones they prefer.

Vocabulary notebooks

Word learning notebooks promote independence and assist memory. They are based on the idea that learners identify the words they want to learn from their own reading or listening, and then record information that will help them use the words in the future. As noted in Chapter 1, words need to be repeated ten or more times to be retained; notebooks allow learners control over the number of times they revisit a word to remember it.

The most common arrangement for a word notebook or journal is column form. The first column should indicate the word, where it was found, and the sample sentence in which it appeared. Then, select about four more column headings, depending on your students' needs and purposes. Use the categories to help you tailor assignments to the level and needs of your students and to change assignments as you cover different aspects of word use.

1st column:

> word, source, and sample sentence (Where did you see or hear the word? Write the sentence in which it appeared.)

Other columns:

> Meaning (give the definition that fits your sample sentence, including a synonym when possible)

Translation

Part of speech (as used in the sample sentence)

Pronunciation (using whatever symbols are clear to you)

Word parts and related word forms (identify the meaningful parts; list any other words related to this one)

Collocations (as in your sample sentence; others indicated by the dictionary)

A picture (draw a picture that will remind you of the word's meaning)

Other occurrences of the word (if you have seen or heard the word elsewhere, describe where)

My practice (give the places or situations where you practiced using the word and the sentences in which you used it)

Example[12]

WORD, SOURCE, AND SAMPLE SENTENCE	MEANING	WORD PARTS	OTHER OCCUR-RENCES	MY PRACTICE
Crisp "There was nothing crisp about the pace or the play at the baseball stadium Monday night." <u>LA Times</u> sports section	Sharp and con-cise	I think it's re-lated to crispy.	I have seen it used to describe lettuce and ce-real.	I asked my teacher, "Are we going to work at a crisp pace today?"

Research suggests that, when left on their own, learners don't get as much from this exercise as they might. For example, they tend to draw most of their target words from textbooks rather than the many other sources that might be valuable (newspapers, campus publications, websites, ads). Learners also have difficulty distinguishing high frequency words from others, and tend to view all words as having equal importance.[13] Provide guidelines about how to select words and review these guidelines regularly. Encourage students to repeat the words in their own sentences, and to focus on a variety of features.

Collect the notebooks every few weeks so you can follow your students' progress and better understand how perceptive they are about noticing what is important. You needn't comment on every entry; providing a few suggestions or guiding questions should be enough (e.g., "This is a very useful word. Listen for it in the news or when people are talking about politics." or "Notice the collocations here.").

Word cards

Word cards are effective because they are convenient and lend themselves to the frequent review that leads to word memory. One possible format: On one side of the card, learners write the target word and its part of speech. On the top half of the other side, they write the word's definition (in English and/or a translation). They also write a sample sentence and a description of its pronunciation. Have students reserve the bottom half of the card for additional notes once they start using the word.

Instruct students to try to add more information about the word each time they practice or observe it. They should note who used the word, its collocations, different sample sentences, and anything else they find interesting about the word's use.[14] Having said that, however, advise learners not to put too much information on the cards. This is only one step in word learning, and too much information will make reviewing the cards cumbersome.[15]

Set aside class time, on a regular basis, for your students to bring their word cards to class. Have students engage in activities such as describing the new words and their sources, quizzing one another, or categorizing the words according to subject, formality, part of speech, or difficulty. Encourage learners to change the order in which they review the cards. Demonstrate effective ways to store and organize them (perhaps in a box with the categories they select, or with the most difficult words in the front).

More important than the number of strategies learners know is the ability to use strategies well. It bears repeating that effective strategy instruction includes frequent modeling, discussions of specifically when and how to apply strategies, and a great deal of guided practice.[16]

KEY CONSIDERATIONS FOR THE CLASSROOM

1 Launch Independent Word Learning in the Classroom

A good vocabulary teacher can influence a student's thoughts about word learning in important ways. Be sure to adopt high standards of word use and acquaint your learners with the satisfying experience of reaching beyond their comfort level. As discussed in Chapter 1, our passive vocabulary develops throughout our lifetime, but our productive lexicon will grow only until it reaches the threshold level of the group in which we participate.[17] A class can be that group, which sets the bar higher than we would set it on our own. Challenging, meaningful interaction and practice will encourage learners to reach for higher levels of word use, first in class and then on their own.

Teachers are always looking for ways to motivate their students within a supportive learning environment. Here are some suggestions:[18]

■ Develop and nurture your own fascination with words and let students see your enthusiasm.

■ Share stories about how word learning has been meaningful or satisfying to you or has opened doors that wouldn't have been opened otherwise.

■ Take your students' learning very seriously. Show them that you care about their progress by being alert to their needs and available to help them.

■ Listen carefully both to students' questions and to their attempts to use new words.

■ Encourage students to take risks. Show them that you respect good questions and that you consider errors a natural feature of learning.

2 Use a Variety of Techniques That Students Can Use on Their Own

Successful word learning is possible when there is ample repetition of new words, and when students start to notice how words relate to one another and how they are used. The following techniques can be useful in class and for students' own use.

▪ Provide opportunities for repetition
  - Use formerly studied words as a natural part of your language in class interaction (e.g., "I will now segue. . ." or "How did the president maintain order during the crisis?").
  - Encourage learners to use recently studied words in classroom questions and discussions (e.g., "Does that mean you will reject papers that aren't double-spaced?").
  - Take the time in class to ask students if they have seen or heard any of the recently studied words and to explain to their classmates how they were used.

▪ Develop alertness to the relationships among words
  - Use word clusters (e.g., semantic maps, word webs).[19]
  - Categorize words in groups (e.g., actions, feelings, settings, personalities).
  - Use antonyms in your classroom comments and assignments (e.g., "Is water a finite or infinite resource?"). This helps in the analysis and understanding of new words.

▪ Develop alertness to word use
  - Talk about the word choices of good authors during reading discussions.
  - Take words or short phrases from good authors or compelling readings and use them as springboards for original expression.[20] Encourage learners to do the same.
  - Use authentic sources to demonstrate the effects of slang when it is used with otherwise formal language (e.g., In a press interview, congressional spokesmen referred to "a bumpy road" and "a no-brainer.").

3 Help Learners Develop Good Word-Learning Habits

Extensive reading is an asset to everyone, at every level, who is interested in learning new words. Though the processes of incidental word learning are not clearly understood, research supports what many of us have experienced: we can learn a lot about words through reading.[21] The best material is at a level that allows the reader to understand at least 95% of the vocabulary. Graded readers are an excellent supplement to course materials because they "provide reading practice, enrich known vocabulary, and provide motivation to continue study through success in use."[22] Explain to students that reading helps them learn new words and helps them learn more about words that they partially know. The mantra of independent word learning is *Read, Read, Read.*

Another effective way for learners to pick up relevant new words is called Community-Based Social Research (CBSR). This is one example of an independent learning project in which students participate in settings of their own choosing and examine the language variety they most want to use. In CBSR, learners select a group of target language speakers with whom they can interact. Then, they systematically observe, record, and reflect upon the characteristics of the language used. The students then discuss their independent investigations in class.[23]

Classroom discussions and projects like CBSR, which give learners specific tasks in authentic settings, are effective ways to help them prepare for a lifetime of independent language learning.

ACTIVITIES

1 Reflections on Relevance

Goal: Learners reflect on various features relevant to word learning (e.g., frequency, regularity, transfer difficulty, pronunciation) and rank words according to difficulty.

Procedure:

1. Conduct a brief class discussion of the features that make words difficult to learn and remember, and write them on the board. Have students consider such factors as frequency, irregular forms, verb transitivity, noun countability, difficult word forms, transfer difficulties, pronunciation, spelling, and similarity to other words.

2. Choose a set of 5–10 target words that have been covered in class.

3. Students work in pairs to rank the target words in order of difficulty, explaining their rationale for each choice.

4. In a class discussion, compare the analyses and talk about the implications. For example, is frequency a feature that makes a word easier or more difficult to learn?

5. Each pair writes a list of the three factors that are most helpful in learning a word and the three most difficult factors of word learning.

2 Tip-offs from the Text

Goal: Students identify textual clues that are most helpful for decoding new words in context.

Procedure:

1. Review with the class the information about using context. (See pages 118–119 of this chapter.)

2. Select a high-interest paragraph from your students' textbook or another source. Select one word that is richly supported with context in the passage. (It is best if the word is repeated more than once.)

3. White out the paragraph on the board and replace the target word with a nonsense word.

4. Students work in pairs, using the context to guess the meaning of the nonsense word, underlining all the clues they find useful.

> **Example**
>
> Harvey Kennedy created the first shoelace and was paid $2,500,000 for his _____. Other people have tried to make money with <u>devices such as</u> a <u>parakeet diaper</u> and a <u>shoe air-conditioner</u>, but these _____ have not been as successful.
>
> Answer: *invention*

5. In a class discussion, students share their insights.

3 Words That Help Review

Goal: Learners identify key words in a reading used in class, and then use them to review the text in a class discussion.

Procedure:

1. For homework, students identify 3–5 words that are important to the main ideas of the reading. (Explain what you mean by "main idea" if necessary.) Dictionaries may be used as needed.

2. In the following class session, students write the words on the board, being careful not to repeat words that their classmates have already written.

3. In a class discussion, briefly review the meanings and pronunciation of the words.

4. Students work in pairs to orally summarize the reading, using as many target words as possible. Encourage them to use different forms of the words in their summaries.

5. Follow up with a whole-class discussion about the reading. Remind students to use the target words (in a variety of forms if possible). Guide them by asking leading questions (e.g., Which character was most persistent about selling the family property? What might be the reason for this persistence?).

Sentence-level follow-up:

Working in pairs, students write 3–5 questions about the reading, using one target word in each sentence (e.g., Why do you think the son was so persistent?). Pairs then ask and answer the questions in a discussion with another pair.

4 Definition Discrimination

Goal: Learners examine the dictionary definitions of similar words and identify the qualities that distinguish them from one another.

Procedure:

1. Review the characteristics of dictionary definitions with the class. (See pages 122–123 of this chapter.)

2. Write about five groups of three near-synonyms on the board. You can use the samples below or create your own.

3. Students work in pairs, first without dictionaries, to identify the key differences between the words. They should consider such factors as how formal and/or specific a word is, and whether it is used most often in a certain domain. Dictionaries may be used to check and complete the answers.

4. In a class discussion, students identify the differences between the words, focusing on the ways that words can differ.

5. In pairs, students select one group of words and write a definition for each of the three words, making the distinctions clear.

Samples of Near-Synonyms:
ignorant, oblivious, uninformed
conceal, hide, camouflage
false, counterfeit, bogus
pleasure, gratification, fun
deceive, dupe, mislead
pain, suffering, grief

5 Dictionary Detectives

Goal: Learners identify and correct errors in a set of sentences. Then they check their dictionaries to see if the relevant grammatical information is provided.

Procedure:
(Students should bring their own dictionaries, bilingual or monolingual, to class for this activity. It is best if each group has a variety of dictionaries to discuss.)

1. Review the information about finding grammatical information in the dictionary. (See pages 121–123 of this chapter and page 68 in Chapter 5.)

2. Write the following sentences on the board, or create similar sentences of your own:

   a. *The doctor <u>suggested</u> me to go home.

   b. *I am <u>fit</u> by a size 7 dress.

   c. *The <u>volcano</u> wasn't working.

   d. *When my family visits, we always <u>hospitalize</u> them.

   e. *She was <u>emphasized</u> by her parents to get a good education.

3. Students work in small groups to identify the errors in the sentences and explain the reasons for the errors.

4. Students then look up each underlined word in their dictionaries to see whether there is information that would help them avoid the errors. If more than one dictionary is available in a group, have students compare the information, translating information in bilingual dictionaries as needed.

5. Students then correct the errors in the sentences without changing meaning.

6. In a class discussion, have students compare findings from various dictionaries and identify the symbols, explanations, and samples that were most helpful.

6 Lexical Scavenger Hunt

Goal: Students find target words in written sources outside the class-room, describe their context, and practice using the words.

Procedure:

(This activity can be used routinely to review target words covered in class.)

1. Provide students with a list of about ten recently studied words.

2. As homework, students select one word from the list and search for instances of it in any printed sources that are not classroom materials (e.g., newspapers, magazines, brochures, Internet sites).

They must bring a copy of the written source to class with the target word identified. Allow at least one week for this assignment.

3. In pairs or small groups, students take turns summarizing the source information and explaining how the target word was used. Remind students to focus on the influences of context and purpose. In a class discussion, review answers, focusing on such features as register, collocations, grammatical features, and multiple meanings.

Sentence-level follow-up:

Within their groups, students exchange target words and sources. Then, in their own words, they restate the main point of the information, using a different form of the target word without changing meaning.

Example

Source: *Wall Street Journal*, "Goldman Sachs Group Inc. lost more than 30% of its value last week during one of the market's most turbulent stretches in recent years."

Restatement: The turbulence of the market led to a loss of 30% for Goldman Sachs.

7 Resourceful Recycling

Goal: Learners use target words to complete an imaginative task, based on a class reading.

Procedure:

1. Select 5–10 target words that are central to an article or story that the class has recently read.
2. Briefly review the target words.
3. Select one of the following activities that relates clearly to the reading.[24] (Variation: you might want to assign different tasks to different groups. Be sure to select activities that fit your reading.)

a. Write an advertisement or a classified ad.

b. Create a radio or TV advertisement.

c. Convert all or part of the article or story into a radio news report.

d. Create a cartoon strip of the story or an event in the article.

e. Discuss how the characters might behave in a different setting.

f. Write a letter from one character to another.

g. Write a diary entry. ["Assume that you are (a specific character). Write your diary entry for (a specific day)."]

h. Write a *TV Guide* summary of the story.

4. Divide the class into pairs or small groups, and instruct them to complete the selected task, using the target words. Circulate as groups are working to help students use the words (and alternate forms) effectively.

5. In a class discussion, focus on the content of the activity, encouraging use of the target words in various forms whenever possible. If you wish, you can draw attention to the use of register, collocations, noun countability, verb forms, and so on.

Notes

Chapter 1

1 This number varies according to how one defines "a word" and many other factors. See Aitchison, *Words in the Mind: An Introduction to the Mental Lexicon*, Schmitt, *Vocabulary in Language Teaching*, and Nation, *Teaching and Learning Vocabulary*, for discussions of research regarding word counts.

2 See Nation, *Teaching and Learning Vocabulary*, and Nation, *Learning Vocabulary in Another Language*, for thorough discussions of incremental word knowledge.

3 See Scott and Nagy, "Developing Word Consciousness," for an overview of research on word consciousness.

4 Examples from Lederer, *Crazy English*.

5 Scott and Nagy, "Developing Word Consciousness," 201.

6 See Scott and Nagy, "Developing Word Consciousness," for an overview of this project, known as The Gift of Words and conducted with elementary school learners whose first language was English.

7 Some of these examples are from Lederer, *Crazy English*.

8 Nation, *Teaching and Learning Vocabulary*, 31; see also Nation, *Learning Vocabulary in Another Language*.

9 For access to several relevant word lists, including the frequency lists mentioned here, see the Compleat Lexical Tutor: http://www.lextutor.ca/ (accessed October 2007).

10 Brown, "Factors Affecting the Acquisition of Vocabulary," 278).

11 For a complete discussion and list of the Academic Word List, see Averil Coxhead's website: http://language.massey.ac.nz/staff/awl/ (accessed October 2007).

12 Corson, *The Lexical Bar*, 78.

13 Laufer, "Why Are Some Words More Difficult Than Others? Some Intralexical Factors That Affect the Learning of Words," 303.

14 For a complete discussion of a word's learning burden, see Nation, *Teaching and Learning Vocabulary*, 33–43.

15 Laufer, "Instructed Second Language Vocabulary Learning: The Fault in the 'Default Hypothesis'," 318, 313.

16 Schmitt, "Second Language Vocabulary Learning."

17 See Webb, "The Effects of Repetition on Vocabulary Knowledge," for a review of the research on repetition in word learning and for an analysis of the types of gains that can be made by repeated encounters with words in context.

18 Pimsleur, "A Memory Schedule," in Nation, *Learning Vocabulary in Another Language*, 76.

19 See Willingham, "Allocating Student Study Time: 'Massed' versus 'Distributed' Practice."

20 Laufer, "Instructed Second Language Vocabulary Learning: The Fault in the 'Default Hypothesis,'" 313.

21 See Laufer, "Instructed Second Language Vocabulary Learning: The Fault in the 'Default Hypothesis," for a discussion of the research supporting this view.

22 See Laufer, "The Development of L2 Lexis in the Expression of the Advanced Learner," 445 for a discussion of the "active vocabulary threshold hypothesis."

23 Brown, *Teaching by Principles: An Interactive Approach to Language Pedagogy.*

Chapter 2

1 Paraphrased from Salomon, *Semantics and Common Sense*, 84–85.

2 Faerch, Haastrup, and Phillipson, "Learner Language and Language Learning," as cited in Laufer, "Why Are Some Words More Difficult Than Others? Some Intralexical Factors That Affect the Learning of Words," 295.

3 See Stahl and Fairbanks, "The Effects of Vocabulary Instruction: A Model-based Meta-analysis," for a meta-analysis of about 70 studies of vocabulary instruction. They concluded that definition information is important, along with contextual information, opportunities to process words, and multiple exposures to words.

4 Beck, McKeown, and Kucan *Bringing Words to Life: Robust Vocabulary Instruction*, viii.

5 Stahl and Fairbanks,"The Effects of Vocabulary Instruction: A Model-based Meta-analysis."

6 Aitchison, *Words in the Mind: An Introduction to the Mental Lexicon*, 91.

7 For a thorough discussion of this view of lexical sets, see Nation, "Learning Vocabulary in Lexical Sets: Dangers and Guidelines."

8 Aitchison, *Words in the Mind: An Introduction to the Mental Lexicon.*

9 Laufer, "What's in a Word That Makes It Hard or Easy: Some Intralexical Factors That Affect the Learning of Words."

10 Laufer, "The Lexical Plight in Second Language Reading."

11 Examples from Bertrand Russell's "conjugation of adjectives," *An Inquiry into Meaning and Truth.*

12 Rich language refers to descriptive and precise language from a variety of interesting spoken and written sources, including extensive reading, reading aloud, academic discussion, and conversation. See Nagy, "Why Vocabulary Instruction Needs to be Long-term and Comprehensive."

13 See Willingham, "Allocating Student Study Time: 'Massed' versus 'Distributed' Practice"; Nation, *Learning Vocabulary in Another Language.*

14 Examples adapted from the research of Visser, "Learning Vocabulary through Underlying Meanings: An Investigation of an Interactive Technique," 17–18.

15 Adapted from McCarthy, *Vocabulary*, 24.

16 Adapted from Hudson, *Word Meaning*, 62.

17 Examples drawn from Wittgenstein, *Philosophical Investigations*, 66, cited in Aitchison, *Words in the Mind: An Introduction to the Mental Lexicon*, 49–50.

18 Beck, Mckeown, and Kucan, *Bringing Words to Life: Robust Vocabulary Instruction*, 13.

Chapter 3

1 McCarthy, *Vocabulary.*

2 For more information about "network building," see Aitchison, *Words in the Mind: An Introduction to the Mental Lexicon.*

3 Lakoff and Johnson, *Metaphors We Live By*, 4, 48.

4 See Schmitt, *Vocabulary in Language Teaching.*

5 Lewis, "Pedagogical Implications of the Lexical Approach," 255

6 Lewis, *The Lexical Approach*; Nattinger and DeCarrico, *Lexical Phrases and Language Teaching.*

7 According to Igor Mel'cuk, quoted in Aitchison, *Words in the Mind: An Introduction to the Mental Lexicon.*

8 See Schmitt, *Vocabulary in Language Teaching*, and Nation, *Learning Vocabulary in Another Language*, for discussions concerning the difficulties involved in teaching and learning collocations.

9 From Compleat Lexical Tutor: http://www.lextutor.ca/scripts/cgi-bin/wwwconcapp.exe.

10 Adapted from Lewis, "Pedagogical Implications of the Lexical Approach," 262–263.

11 Adapted from McCarthy *Vocabulary*, 15.

Chapter 4

1 See Singleton, *Language and the Lexicon,* for a discussion of the interaction between syntax and vocabulary from the perspectives of several linguistic schools of thought.

2 Nagy, "On the Role of Context in First and Second Language Vocabulary Learning"; Landau and Gleitman, *Language and Experience: Evidence from the Blind Child.*

3 Katz, Bakerand, and MacNamara, *What's in a Name? A Study of How Children Learn Common and Proper Nouns,"* cited in Nagy, "On the Role of Context in First and Second Language Vocabulary Learning."

4 Nagy, "On the Role of Context in First and Second Language Vocabulary Learning"; Naigles, "Children Use Syntax to Learn Verb Meanings."

5 Examples from Swan and Smith, *Learner English: A Teacher's Guide to Interference and Other Problems.*

6 The major word classes are nouns, verbs, adjectives, and adverbs; they carry most of the content of the sentence. The minor word classes, also called function words, include auxiliary verbs, prepositions, pronouns, determiners, and conjunctions. See Celce-Murcia and Larsen-Freeman, *The Grammar Book: An ESL/EFL Teacher's Course,* for more information.

7 For example, in the sentence, *Qué guapa mujer! (What a good-looking woman!), guapa* is an adjective. In the sentence, *Guapa, necesitas firmar este documento (Good-looking, you need to sign this document), guapa* is a noun.

8 Research suggests that nouns are the easiest to learn, adverbs are the hardest, and verbs and adjectives fall somewhere in between. See Schmitt, *Vocabulary in Language Teaching,* for a review of these studies.

9 See Hinkel, *Teaching Academic ESL Writing: Practical Techniques in Vocabulary and Grammar,* 106, for a more extensive list of structural patterns and for practical suggestions concerning countable and uncountable academic nouns.

10 See Celce-Murcia and Larsen-Freeman, *The Grammar Book: An ESL/EFL Teacher's Course,* 347–348, for a complete list of these constraints on passive voice.

11 Celce-Murcia and Larsen-Freeman, *The Grammar Book: An ESL/EFL Teacher's Course.*

12 Examples taken from Celce-Murcia and Larsen-Freeman, *The Grammar Book: An ESL/EFL Teacher's Course,* 648–649. See this section for a discussion of meaning differences implied by the choice of infinitive or gerund.

13 Biber, Johansson, Leech, Conrad, and Finegan, *Longman Grammar of Spoken and Written English.*

14 Celce-Murcia and Larsen-Freeman, *The Grammar Book: An ESL/EFL Teacher's Course*, 36.

15 Aitchison, *Words in the Mind: An Introduction to the Mental Lexicon.*

16 Example from Rutherford, *Second Language Grammar: Learning and Teaching*, 88.

17 Nation, *Teaching and Learning Vocabulary.*

18 Celce-Murcia and Larsen-Freeman, *The Grammar Book: An ESL/EFL Teacher's Course.*

Chapter 5

1 Many of these examples are from Lederer, *Crazy English.*

2 See Laufer, "The Lexical Plight in Second Language Reading," and "What's in a Word That Makes It Hard or Easy: Some Intralexical Factors That Affect the Learning of Words," for more thorough discussions of this tendency, known as "deceptive transparency."

3 See Stahl and Nagy, *Teaching Word Meanings*, 29–32 for a discussion of the number of words known by children.

4 Aitchinson, *Words in the Mind: An Introduction to the Mental Lexicon.*

5 Schmitt, *Vocabulary in Language Teaching.*

6 Schmitt and Zimmerman, ."Derivative Word Forms: What Do Learners Know?" 162.

7 See Nation, *Learning Vocabulary in Another Language*, 275–278, for a thorough discussion of the teaching and testing of these skills.

8 See Stahl and Nagy, T*eaching Word Meanings*, 166–172, for complete frequency lists of roots and affixes.

9 McCarthy, *Vocabulary*, 5.

10 For a thorough overview of spelling rules including online handouts, see the Purdue University OWL website: http://owl.english.purdue.edu/.

11 Turner, "Spelling Final "y" before a Suffix." http://www.uottawa.ca/academic/arts/writcent/hypergrammar/spfiny.html.

12 Celce-Murcia, *The Grammar Book: An ESL/EFL Teacher's Course*, 47.

13 Stahl and Nagy, *Teaching Word Meanings.*

14 For more details about the factors affecting the ease of word part learning, see Nation, *Learning Vocabulary in Another Language*, 271.

15 Saragi, "A Study of English Suffixes," as cited in Nation, *Teaching and Learning Vocabulary*, 169.

16 Stahl and Nagy, *Teaching Word Meanings*, 166.

17 Nation, *Teaching and Learning Vocabulary*, 45; Nation, *Learning Vocabulary in Another Language.*

18 Corson, *The Lexical Bar.*

19 Laufer, " Why Are Some Words More Difficult Than Others? Some Intralexical Factors That Affect the Learning of Words."

20 Nation, *Learning Vocabulary in Another Language*, 275.

21 Adapted from Yorkey, *Springboards: Interacting in English*, 12.

22 Adapted from McCarthy, *Vocabulary*, 6.

Chapter 6

1 McCarthy, *Vocabulary*, 61.

2 Halliday, McIntosh, and Strevens, *The Linguistic Science and Language Teaching*, 302, in Laufer, "Why Are Some Words More Difficult Than Others? Some Intralexical Factors That Affect the Learning of Words."

3 For a more complete discussion of the types of register variation, see Schmitt, *Vocabulary in Language Teaching*, 31–35.

4 Scarcella & Rumberger, "Academic English Key to Long-term Success in School," 1.

5 Corson, *The Lexical Bar*.

6 Burke, *The English Teacher's Companion*.

7 For a detailed discussion of academic vocabulary and the Academic Word List, see Coxhead, "A New Academic Word List."

8 Nation, *Learning Vocabulary in Another Language*; Coxhead, "A New Academic Word List."

9 Corson, *The Lexical Bar*, suggests that enormous numbers of students have limited access to education because of a "lexical bar," or the inability to understand and use academic vocabulary, imposed in part because of social inequities in the schools.

10 You can find up-to-date lists of slang by searching on the Internet for "slang dictionaries."

11 Andersson and Trudgill, *Bad Language*, 81–82.

12 Access and Key: Oxford University Press, *Oxford English Dictionary Online*. http://dictionary.oed.com/

13 Firth and Wagner, "On Discourse, Communication, and (Some) Fundamental Concepts in SLA Research."

14 Van Lier, *Interaction in the Language Curriculum: Awareness, Autonomy and Authenticity*.

15 Adapted from McCarthy, *Vocabulary*, 65.

16 Adapted from Salomon, *Semantics and Common Sense*, 152.

Chapter 7

1 Robinson, *Travel and Leisure*, cited by van Lier, "Perception and Awareness: An Ecological Perspective."

2 This is the self-assessment scale used in the textbook series, *Inside Reading: The Academic Word List in Context*, Oxford University Press, 2009.

3 Liu and Nation, "Factors Affecting Guessing Vocabulary in Context."

4 Stahl and Nagy, *Teaching Word Meanings*, 175; See Laufer, "The Lexical Plight in Second Language Reading," Nation, *Learning Vocabulary in Another Language*, and Stahl and Nagy, *Teaching Word Meanings*, for discussions of guessing words in context and word learning.

5 Bensoussan and Laufer, "Lexical Guessing in Context in EFL Reading Comprehension."

6 Haynes, "Patterns and Perils of Guessing in Second Language Reading."

7 Adapted from Burgmeier, Eldred, and Zimmerman, *Lexis: Academic Vocabulary Study*, 190–191.

8 Stahl and Nagy, *Teaching Word Meanings*.

9 *Oxford English Dictionary*

10 For a complete discussion of the "look-up process," see Scholfield, "Using the English Dictionary for Comprehension."

11 See Hudson, *Word Meaning*, for a discussion of classifiers and distinguishers.

12 Adapted from Lubliner *Getting Into Words: Vocabulary Instruction That Strengthens Comprehension*, 110.

13 McCrostie, "Examining Learner Vocabulary Notebooks."

14 This format for word cards is adapted from Schmitt and Schmitt, *Focus on Vocabulary*.

15 Nation, *Learning Vocabulary in Another Language*.

16 Stahl and Nagy, *Teaching Word Meanings*, 158.

17 Laufer, "The Development of L2 Lexis in the Expression of the Advanced Learner," 445.

18 See Dornyei, *Motivational Strategies in the Language Classroom*, 31–49, for a thorough discussion of motivational conditions.

19 Burke, *The English Teacher's Companion*, 112.

20 Adapted from Scott and Nagy, "Developing Word Consciousness," 210.

21 For more about this topic, see Stahl and Nagy, *Teaching Word Meanings*, and Zimmerman, "Do Reading and Interactive Vocabulary Instruction Make a Difference? An Empirical Study."

22 Nation, *Learning Vocabulary in Another Language*, 162. See this source for a complete discussion of graded readers.

23 Peirce, "Social Identity, Investment, and Language Learning."

24 The original list of post-reading activities is from Arline Burgmeier, CATESOL.

References

Aitchison, Jean. *Words in the Mind: An Introduction to the Mental Lexicon.* 3rd Edition. Oxford: Blackwell Publishing, 2003.

Andersson, Lars-Gunnar, and Peter Trudgill. *Bad Language.* Oxford: Basil Blackwell Ltd., 1990.

Beck, Isabel L., Margaret G. McKeown, and Linda Kucan. *Bringing Words to Life: Robust Vocabulary Instruction.* New York: Guilford Press, 2002.

Bensoussan, Marsha, and Batia Laufer. "Lexical Guessing in Context in EFL Reading Comprehension." *Journal of Research in Reading* 7, no. 1 (1984): 15–32.

Biber, Douglas, Stig Johansson, Geoffrey Leech, Susan Conrad, and Edward Finegan. *Longman Grammar of Spoken and Written English.* White Plains, NY: Longman, 1999.

Brown, Cheryl. "Factors Affecting the Acquisition of Vocabulary." In *Second Language Reading and Vocabulary Learning,* edited by Thomas Huckin, Margot Hayne, and James Coady, 263–286. Norwood, NJ: Ablex Publishing, 1993.

Brown, H. Douglas. *Teaching by Principles: An Interactive Approach to Language Pedagogy.* 2nd Edition. Englewood Cliffs, NJ: Prentice Hall Regents, 2001.

Burgmeier, Arline. *Paper presented at the CATESOL State Conference.* Oakland, CA, April 1986.

Burgmeier, Arline, Gerry Eldred, and Cheryl B. Zimmerman. *Lexis: Academic Vocabulary Study.* Englewood Cliffs, NJ: Prentice Hall, 1991.

Burke, Jim. *The English Teacher's Companion.* Portsmouth, NH: Boynton/Cook Heinemann, 2003.

Celce-Murcia, Marianne, and Diane Larsen-Freeman. *The Grammar Book: An ESL/ EFL Teacher's Course.* 2nd Edition. Boston: Heinle and Heinle Publishers, 1999.

Cobb, Thomas. *The Compleat Lexical Tutor.* 2006. http://www.lextutor.ca.

Corson, David. *The Lexical Bar.* Oxford: Pergamon Press, 1985.

Coxhead, Averil. "A New Academic Word List." *TESOL Quarterly* 34, no. 2 (2000): 213–238.

Coxhead, Averil. *The Academic Word List.* http://language.massey.ac.nz/staff/ awl/index.shtml (accessed October 12, 2007).

Dornyei, Zoltan. *Motivational Strategies in the Language Classroom.* Cambridge: Cambridge University Press, 2001.

Firth, Alan, and Johannes Wagner. "On Discourse, Communication, and (Some) Fundamental Concepts in SLA Research." *Modern Language Journal* 81, no. 3 (1997): 277–300.

Greaves, Christopher. *Web Concordancer*. n.d. http://www.edict.com.hk/concordance/default.htm.

Haynes, Margot. "Patterns and Perils of Guessing in Second Language Reading." In *Second Language Reading and Vocabulary Learning*, edited by Thomas Huckin, Margot Hayne, and James Coady, 46-64. Norwood, NJ: Ablex Publishing, 1993.

Haywood, Sandra. *University of Nottingham Website for Academic Vocabulary Study*. 2003. http://www.nottingham.ac.uk/~alzsh3/acvocab/ .

Hinkel, Eli. *Teaching Academic ESL Writing: Practical Techniques in Vocabulary and Grammar*. Mahwah, NJ: Lawrence Erlbaum Associates, 2004.

Hudson, Richard. *Word Meaning*. New York: Routledge, 1995.

Lakoff, George, and Mark Johnson. *Metaphors We Live By*. Chicago: University of Chicago Press, 1980.

Landau, Barbara, and Lila R. Gleitman. *Language and Experience: Evidence from the Blind Child*. Cambridge, MA: Harvard University Press, 1985.

Laufer, Batia. "Why Are Some Words More Difficult Than Others? Some Intra-lexical Factors That Affect the Learning of Words." *IRAL* 28 (1990): 293–307.

Laufer, Batia. "The Development of L2 Lexis in the Expression of the Advanced Learner." *The Modern Language Journal* 75, no. 4 (1991): 440–448.

Laufer, Batia. "The Lexical Plight in Second Language Reading." In *Second Language Vocabulary Acquisition: A Rationale for Pedagogy*, edited by James Coady and Thomas Huckin, 20–34. Cambridge: Cambridge University Press, 1997.

Laufer, Batia. "What's in a Word That Makes It Hard or Easy: Some Intralexical Factors That Affect the Learning of Words." In *Vocabulary: Description, Acquisition and Pedagogy*, edited by Norbert Schmitt and Michael McCarthy 140–155. Cambridge: Cambridge University Press, 1997.

Laufer, Batia. "Instructed Second Language Vocabulary Learning: The Fault in the 'Default Hypothesis.'" In *Investigations in Instructed Second Language Acquisition*, edited by Alex Housen and Michel Pierrard, 311–332. New York: Mouton de Gruyter, 2005.

Lederer, Richard. *Crazy English*. New York: Simon and Schuster, 1989.

Lewis, Michael. *The Lexical Approach*. Hove, England: Language Teaching Publications, 1993.

Lewis, Michael. "Pedagogical Implications of the Lexical Approach." In *Second Language Vocabulary Acquisition: A Rationale for Pedagogy*, edited by James Coady and Thomas Huckin, 255–270. Cambridge: Cambridge University Press, 1997.

Liu, Na, and I. S. P. Nation. "Factors Affecting Guessing Vocabulary in Context." *RELC Journal* 16 (1985): 35–42.

Lubliner, Shira. *Getting Into Words: Vocabulary Instruction That Strengthens Comprehension*. Baltimore: Paul H. Brookes Publishing, 2005.

McCarthy, Michael. *Vocabulary*. Oxford: Oxford University Press, 1990.

McCrostie, James. "Examining Learner Vocabulary Notebooks." *ELT Journal* 61, no. 3 (2007): 246–255.

Morley, Catherine. "Collocation Pelmanism." BBC-British Council website for Teaching English vocabulary activities. http://www.teachingenglish.org.uk/try/vocabtry/pelmanism.shtml.

Nagy, William E. "On the Role of Context in First and Second Language Vocabulary Learning." In *Vocabulary: Description, Acquisition and Pedagogy*, edited by Norbert Schmitt and Michael McCarthy, 64-83. Cambridge: Cambridge University Press, 1997.

Nagy, William E. "Why Vocabulary Instruction Needs to be Long-term and Comprehensive." In *Teaching and Learning Vocabulary: Bringing Research to Practice*, edited by Elfrieda H. Hiebert and Michael L. Kamil, 27–44. Mahwah, NJ: Lawrence Earlbaum Associates, 2005.

Naigles, Letitia. "Children Use Syntax to Learn Verb Meanings." *Journal of Child Language* 17 (1990): 357–74.

Natinger, James R. and Jeanette S. DeCarrico. *Lexical Phrases and Language Teaching*. Oxford: Oxford University Press, 1992.

Nation, I. S. P. *Teaching and Learning Vocabulary*. New York: Newbury House, 1990.

Nation, I. S. P. *Learning Vocabulary in Another Language*. Cambridge: Cambridge University Press, 2001.

Nation, Paul. "Learning Vocabulary in Lexical Sets: Dangers and Guidelines." *TESOL Journal* 9, no. 2 (2000): 6–10.

Oxford University Press. *Oxford English Dictionary Online*. http://dictionary.oed.com/ (accessed September 13, 2007).

Peirce, Bonnie Norton. "Social Identity, Investment, and Language Learning." *TESOL Quarterly* 29, no. 1 (1995): 9–31.

Purdue OWL, "Online Writing Lab." http://owl.english.purdue.edu/owl/ (accessed September 12, 2007).

Robinson, Roxana.. "New Zealand's Natural Wonders." *Travel and Leisure*, July 2004, 142–152.

Russell, Bertrand. *An Inquiry into Meaning and Truth*. Baltimore: Penguin, 1962.

Rutherford, William E. *Second Language Grammar: Learning and Teaching*. New York: Longman, 1987.

Salomon, Louis Bernard. *Semantics and Common Sense*. New York: Holt Rinehart and Winston, 1966.

Scarcella, Robin, and Russell W. Rumberger. "Academic English Key to Long-term Success in School." *University of California Linguistic Minority Research Institute Newsletter* 9, Summer 2000, 1–2.

Schmitt, Diane, and Norbert Schmitt. *Focus on Vocabulary*. White Plains, New York: Longman, 2005.

Schmitt, Norbert. *Vocabulary in Language Teaching*. Cambridge: Cambridge University Press, 2000.

Schmitt, Norbert. "Second Language Vocabulary Learning." Lecture presented at a seminar for the TESOL Club, California State University, Fullerton, April 2007.

Schmitt, Norbert, and Cheryl Boyd Zimmerman."Derivative Word Forms: What Do Learners Know?" *TESOL Quarterly* 36, no. 2 (2002): 145–171.

Scholfield, Phil J. "Using the English Dictionary for Comprehension." *TESOL Quarterly* 16, no. 2 (1982): 185–194.

Scott, Judith A., and William E. Nagy. "Developing Word Consciousness." In *Vocabulary Instruction: Research to Practice*, edited by James F. Baumann and Edward J. Kame'enui, 201–217. New York: Guilford Press, 2004.

Singleton, David. *Language and the Lexicon: An Introduction*. London: Arnold, 2000.

Sokmen, Anita J. *Common Threads: An Interactive Vocabulary Builder*. Englewood Cliffs, NJ: Prentice Hall, 1991.

Stahl, Steven A., and Marilyn M. Fairbanks. "The Effects of Vocabulary Instruction: A Model-based Meta-analysis." *Review of Educational Research* 56, no. 1 (1986): 198672–1986110.

Stahl, Steven A., and William E. Nagy. T*eaching Word Meanings*. Mahwah, NJ: Lawrence Erlbaum Associates, 2006.

Swan, Michael and Bernard Smith, eds. *Learner English: A Teacher's Guide to Interference and Other Problems*. Cambridge: Cambridge University Press, 1987.

Turner, Dorothy. "Spelling Final "y" before a Suffix." University of Ottawa, Writing Center. http://www.uottawa.ca/academic/arts/writcent/hypergrammar/spfiny.html (accessed June 29, 2007).

Tyler, Andrea, and William Nagy. "The Acquisition of English Derivational Morphology." *Journal of Memory and Language* 28 (1989): 649–667.

Van Lier, Leo. *Interaction in the Language Curriculum: Awareness, Autonomy and Authenticity*. New York: Longman, 1996.

Van Lier, Leo. "Perception and Awareness: An Ecological Perspective." *Paper presented at the conference of the Association for Language Awareness, Lleida, Spain*, July 2004.

Visser, Annette. "Learning Vocabulary through Underlying Meanings: An Investigation of an Interactive Technique." *RELC Journal* 21, no. 1 (1990): 11–28.

Webb, Stuart. "The Effects of Repetition on Vocabulary Knowledge." *Applied Linguistics* 28, no. 1(2007): 46–65.

Willingham, Daniel T. (2002). "Allocating Student Study Time: 'Massed' versus 'Distributed' Practice." *American Educator*, Summer 2002. http://www.aft. org/pubs-reports/american_educator/summer2002/askcognitivescientist. html (accessed February 6, 2007).

Yorkey, Richard. *Springboards: Interacting in English.* Massachusetts: Addison-Wesley, 1984.

Zimmerman, Cheryl B. "Do Reading and Interactive Vocabulary Instruction Make a Difference? An Empirical Study." *TESOL Quarterly* 31, no. 1 (1997): 121–140.

Zimmerman, Cheryl B., ed. *Inside Reading: The Academic Word List in Context.* Four levels. New York: Oxford University Press, 2009.

Answer Key

Chapter 2

1 Word Ranking and Reshuffling
   Answers will vary.
2 Reflecting on Meaning
   Answers will vary. Some examples:
   1a. You can release energy, release a
       movie, release hostages, etc.
   1b. Release is a transitive verb. In this
       sentence it is used without an object.
   2a. Soil, farmland, a town, and clothing
       can all be saturated.
   2b. A saturated market is one in which
       one area of commerce has too many
       products available, so prices are low
       and buyers have many choices.
   2c. Answers will vary.
   2d. Answers will vary.
4 Human or Not? Part A
   Answers will vary. Some examples:
   People: man/woman, male/female, produce, train, refined, traditional, kind,
   harsh, domesticated, conservative
   Animals: male/female, species, breed,
   produce, train, domesticated
   Things: male/female, species, medley,
   garnish, breed, cultivate, produce,
   train, decorate, refine, traditional,
   eternal, conservative
5 Human or Not? Part B
   People: blond, brunette
   Animals: breed, feed (noun)
   Both: to be born; reproduce; eat; groom
   (verb)
6 Meanings with "Shades" and Connotations
   Positive for short, petite; Negative,
   dumpy
   Positive for large, generously proportioned; Negative, bulky
   Positive for small, diminutive; Negative,
   stunted
   Positive for quiet, serene; Negative, docile
7 How STRONG are these words?
   displeased/incensed: variations include
   annoyed, irritated, angry
   competent/expert: variations include
   capable, skilled, proficient
   pleased/elated: variations include
   happy, delighted, thrilled

unpleasant/dreadful: variations include
   unspeakable, bad, awful
   remove/annihilate: variations include
   destroy, demolish, tear down
8 Where are the boundaries?
   Answers will vary; consult a dictionary
   as needed.

Chapter 3

1 Collocation Opposites
   Opposites include: simple task / hard;
   simple solution / elaborate; general idea /
   specific; general knowledge / specialized
2 Computer Collocate Comprehension
   Collocates include: geek, froze, shut
   down, screen, keyboard, log off, reboot,
   switch off, log on, crash, turn off, turn
   on, desktop, laptop.
   Other answers will vary.
3 Clues for Collocation Collection
   Answers will vary. Some examples:
   a. business meeting (adjectives): long,
      tedious, informative, important, pro-
      ductive, efficient, disorganized
   b. how one might sing (adverbs): beau-
      tifully, well, loudly, lustily, gently,
      softly, cheerfully
   c. possible actions of a professor
      (verbs): lecture, inform, discipline, cor-
      rect, discuss, request, demand, expect
   d. what can be done with data (verbs): an-
      alyze, scrutinize, examine, criticize,
      collect, capture, enter, access, retrieve,
      manage
4 Metaphorical Ups and Downs
   Answers will vary. Some examples:
   Up: We hit a peak; I'm feeling up or
   upbeat; My spirits rose; I'm on cloud
   nine; rise to the top; high standards;
   upstanding citizen; upright
   Down: I'm feeling down; My spirits
   sank; I'm down in the dumps; Don't
   stoop to that; low standards; under-
   handed; low-down thing to do
5 Why can't you say…?: Connotation
   versus Animacy
   a. Commanded has a negative
      connotation.
   b. Incurable is animate; it's not used for
      objects like cars.

c. Provoked has a negative connotation.

d. Inspired has a positive connotation.

e. Operated is used in surgery, not in sewing.

6 Functions of Phrases

Possible functions: express a greeting or a closing, express disagreement, introduce an example or an exception, summarize, qualify, or limit the scope of a topic

LEXICAL PHRASE	FUNCTION
By and large	summarize
That is,	introduce an example
Hold your horses!	express disagreement
For the most part	introduce an example or an exception
How ya doing?	express a greeting
In essence,	summarize or limiting the scope of a topic
While it may be true that…	introduce an example or an exception
See you later.	express a closing
On the other hand…	introduce an exception

7 Idioms and Lexical Phrases

a. Life is not as rosy as you might think.

b. The kids were cracking jokes.

c. It's raining cats and dogs.

d. Spare the rod, spoil the child.

e. Blood is thicker than water.

f. That goes without saying.

g. When in Rome, do as the Romans do.

Others answers will vary.

Chapter 4

3 Countability Confusion

Answers will vary. Some examples:

After he majored in business, he started a business selling software.

I try not to eat too much cheese, but three cheeses that
I really like are Provolone, Brie, and White Cheddar.

They don't drink wine every night, but they always choose a nice red wine when they are eating beef.

We don't have a lot of time to waste. I don't know how many times I have told you that!!

I had to write so many papers for my history class that I had to buy extra paper.

They say that chocolate is healthy, but if I ate a chocolate every time I wanted one, I would probably be sick.

We have four glasses that are made of blue glass.

We met for a coffee at the coffee shop.

I take aspirin because an aspirin a day is good for your heart.

I have such long hair that I had to buy a hair clip to keep it out of my face.

4 How regular is verb regularity?

examine, examined, examined

know, knew, known

say, said, said

choose, chose, chosen

entitle (to), entitled (to), entitled (to)

6 Why can't you say…?

a. I want my mother to come.

b. They forced him to confess.

c. I understood that I was the winner.

d. The interviewer insisted that I stay for lunch.

e. They disagreed about going to the movie.

f. He enjoys playing the piano.

7 More about That Verb

He abolished.

Incomplete; extension must be a noun or noun phrase.

He reacted.

Complete; extension may begin with against or to.

He advocated.

Incomplete; extension must be a noun or noun phrase.

He concentrated.

Complete; extension may begin with on.

Answers for ways to extend the sentences will vary.

Chapter 5

1 Word Surgery A (Dividing Words into Parts)

Answers may vary.

PREFIXES	ROOTS	SUFFIXES
im-	poss	-ible
X	care	-ful; -ly
X	work; force	X
X	benefic	-ial
re-	ward	-ing

Sentence-level follow-up:

Answers will vary. Some examples:
Student #1: I find it impossible to decide what my dream job will be, but I
will choose it carefully. I will choose a
job that is financially beneficial both to
my family and I hope it is one that will
be personally rewarding also.
Student #2: It is an impossibility for me
to decide about my dream job, but I
don't want to be careless about the
choice. I would like to have a job that
has financial benefits for my family,
and I hope that it has personal rewards
also.
2 Practice Producing Parts
Answers will vary. Some examples:
Verbs: to have; to house; to harbor; to
own; to move into; to equip; to eat (in
the home); to earn (money to buy…);
to encourage; to employ
Nouns: hovel; hut; house; housing;
hotel; haven; ownership; oven; man-
sion; manor; machines; employment
Adjectives: humble; ostentatious;
mobile; muddy; miserable; energy-
efficient; eager; encouraging
Adverbs: humbly; happily; overly
(expensive); miserably (if you miss the
rent); eagerly
3 Compound Contest
Book: notebook; bookcase; bookend;
bookstore; textbook; cookbook.
Card: cardboard; card table; card game;
playing cards; credit card; cardholder
Table: tablecloth; table saw; card table;
coffee table; end table; dining table;
tabletop; table tennis; tableware;
table wine
Work: housework; homework;
workplace; workout; workaholic;
workbench; workbook.
4 Change Begets Change

CHANGE NOUNS TO ADJECTIVES	
Noun	Adjective
phoTOGraphy	PHOtographed

CHANGE VERBS TO NOUNS	
Verb	Noun
reCORD	REcord
REcognize	recogNItion

CHANGE VERBS TO NOUNS TO NAME A PERSON WHO DOES THIS ACTION	
Verb	Noun
liberate	liberator
educate	educator

6 Tell It in Reverse
Possible equivalents: dislike, irrelevant,
uninteresting, unbelievable, disturbing, disgusting, unpleasant, unable to –,
inappropriate, unrealistic, illogical,
unreliable, undependable, (makes me)
uncomfortable, unappealing, unintelligent, incapable of –, disagreeable.
Sentence-level follow-up:
Answers will vary. One example:
My boyfriend is wonderful! I like him
very much. His conversation is relevant
and interesting, and I always believe
what he says. I think his stories are clev-
er, and unique, even though my father
doesn't like them. In addition, I think he
is logical and reliable, and I can always
count on him. He is very intelligent and
I think he is very capable of supporting
me and our family. Finally, we are very
compatible and I like being with him!
(My father is the one who is disagreeable!)

Chapter 6

2 Computer Components
a. compounds based on familiar words:
download; broadband; domain name;
chat room, motherboard
b. words borrowed from another
domain: migrate; mouse
c. entirely new words: gigabyte; Ethernet
3 Euphemistic Expression
Answers will vary. Some examples:
Die: pass on; pass away; pass; breathe
your last; depart this life; expire
Toilet: restroom; washroom; bathroom;
lavatory; powder room; little boy's/
girls' room
Drunk: intoxicated; inebriated; under
the influence; tipsy; silly
Insane: eccentric; unconventional;
peculiar; a little off center; not with it;
different
Fat: big boned, plump, healthy, stout
Old person: elder, senior citizen, senior,
advanced in age.

Note: Use a Thesaurus to expand this list.

4 Register Transformations: Coworker Complaint
Some answers will vary. Some examples (bold answers do not vary):

Hey, Amy!	Dear Amy
stressed out	nervous; upset; having a hard time
hafta	**have to** (must)
let off some steam	vent; be honest; be open
driving me crazy	is very upsetting/ disturbing
I don't get it!	This is very unusual behavior; I don't understand
slob	is very untidy; disorganized
junk	belongings; possessions
gonna	**going to**
makes a mess	does not clean up after herself; isn't neat or clean
slopped up	was untidy
How gross!	Oh my!
kid	to speak indirectly or diplomatically
dirty work	unpleasant tasks
Yech!	How unpleasant!
dropped a lot of hints	tried to be diplomatic; politely mentioned my concerns
"a neat freak"	an obsessively or fanatically tidy or clean person
Help!	I hope you can be of assistance.

Sentence-level follow-up: Answers will vary.

7 Formal Counterparts

FREQUENT COMMON COLLOQUIAL WORDS	FORMAL COUNTERPARTS
could of, would of, should of	could have, would have, should have
cute	adorable
wanna	want to
kid (a young person)	child; youngster; young person; newborn; infant; toddler; pre-schooler; adolescent; offspring.
cheap (an adjective to describe a person)	miserly; parsimonious
haggle	negotiate; bargain; barter
kind of, sort of	rather; somewhat; to a degree
snoop	investigate; explore; probe

Chapter 7

5 Dictionary Detectives
  a. Suggested is intransitive; follow it with a that-clause.
  b. Fit cannot be made passive because it is intransitive.
  c. Volcano collocates with erupts or is active.
  d. There is no verb form for hospitable; We are hospitable to them.
  e. Emphasized is transitive. The base sentence here is Her parents emphasized a good education. The passive form would be Education was emphasized by her parents.

Index